FINAL CUT PRO 4
ON THE SPOT

FINAL CUT PRO 4

ON THE SPOT

TIME-SAVING TIPS & SHORTCUTS
FROM THE PROS

by **Richard Harrington**
& **Abba Shapiro**

DV

Digital Video

EXPERT SERIES

CMP**Books**

San Francisco CA • New York NY • Lawrence KS

Published by CMP Books
an imprint of CMP Media LLC
Main office: 600 Harrison Street, San Francisco, CA 94107 USA
Tel: 415-947-6615; fax: 415-947-6015
Editorial office: 4601 West 6th St, Suite B, Lawrence, KS 66049
 USA
www.cmpbooks.com
email: books@cmp.com

Technical editor: Tom Wolsky
Cover design: Damien Castaneda

Distributed to the book trade in the U.S. by:
Publishers Group West
1700 Fourth Street
Berkeley, CA 94710
1-800-788-3123

Distributed in Canada by:
Jaguar Book Group
100 Armstrong Avenue
Georgetown, Ontario M6K 3E7 Canada
905-877-4483

For individual orders and for information on special discounts for quantity orders, please contact:
CMP Books Distribution Center, 6600 Silacci Way, Gilroy, CA 95020
Tel: 1-800-500-6875 or 408-848-3854; fax: 408-848-5784
email: cmp@rushorder.com; Web: www.cmpbooks.com

04 05 06 07 08   5 4 3 2 1

ISBN: 1-57820-231-0

Dedication

This book is dedicated to my wife, Meghan, and our family.
—Richard Harrington

This book is dedicated to my wife, Lisa; our children, Daniel and Ian;
and our families.
—Abba Shapiro

Table of Contents

Introduction

Why did we write this book? We love this application. We use it ourselves almost every day to edit and to create programs for our clients. We teach Final Cut Pro classes, give lectures, and consult one on one. And you know what makes us feel really good? When people learn a new trick or tip, smile, and say, "Wow!"

We still learn new tricks every day, and we still smile and say, "Wow!" We wanted to pass that excitement along. As much as we love this program, we can't teach everywhere, we can't answer the phone every night at 3 a.m. (our wives would kill us), and we can only get across so many tips in the time allotted to us at conferences.

So we wrote a book. The idea was to give the reader the cream off the top of the milk—just the good stuff. Final Cut Pro is a great program, with tons of features and shortcuts; the problem is separating the cream from the skim milk.

If you read every tech document on the web, perused every page of the manual, attended all of the Apple certification courses, and hung out with all the other FCP uber-geeks, not to mention the Final Cut Pro people at Apple, you'd have a bounty of knowledge (trust us, we have and we do). But you have a life, a job, and no time to dig to find those gems.

If you're impatient, on a deadline, or just can't stand to look at another 'Getting Started with Final Cut Pro' book, this book is for you.

We've both used Final Cut Pro from the beginning; in fact, we've got more than 20 years combined experience with nonlinear editing and 40 years of hands-on Apple usage. And we've distilled that knowledge into this book, giving you the best tidbits and secrets we have.

All we ask is that you tell your friends about this book, and that when you win your first Oscar/Emmy (or make your first million dollars), you remember us—or, better yet, just smile and thank us at the next NAB, DV, or Apple trade show.

Who Is This Book For?

If you've edited nonlinear video for a while and feel comfortable editing, you can get a lot out of this book. If you're a seasoned editor, we may help break you of some extremely slow habits and show you some really cool techniques. This book will help you move to a higher level.

If you've never opened the manual, read another Final Cut Pro book, or taken a training class, don't start here. You must learn to walk before you can run. If you're a "newbie," this book may leave you a bit overwhelmed. Buy it anyway, but read it after you've had some walking lessons.

With that said, don't try to read the book linearly. Shop for ideas, jump around a lot, and work your way through the chapters you need most. We've left extra space by the tips so you can jot down your own notes. If you're a mobile editor, this book should fit nicely in your bag. Hit a tough spot, and just pull the book out when the client leaves the room to check for a new idea or a troubleshooting tip. Have a few minutes to kill, read a tip. We bet you'll return to the application with some new ideas and new energy.

If you're looking for the little sidebars or tips in the margins, there aren't any. This whole book is filled with more than 350 tips. Get reading already–you've got a deadline to make.

–Richard Harrington and Abba Shapiro

Updates

Want to receive e-mail news updates for *Final Cut Pro 4 On the Spot*? Send a blank e-mail to fcp4spot@news.cmpbooks.com. We will do our best to keep you informed of software updates and enhancements, new tips, and other FCP-related resources. Further, if you would like to contribute to the effort by reporting any errors or by posting your own tips, please contact the authors at www.finalcutprohelp.com.

ON THE SPOT

Plugging In
Mastering Final Cut Pro's Interface

So you want to be fast? A virtuoso of the Final Cut Pro keyboard? A concert pianist doesn't see the piano as a tool but as a conduit for the music. In the same way, Final Cut Pro is a conduit for your show and your creativity. Mastering the interface will keep you from stumbling in the dark, hitting the wrong keys, and making a lot of noise. You have to know what all your tools do, where to find them, and how to access their power instantly.

Over time, you'll gain confidence with all the controls. You want to be able to make the interface "disappear," which will allow you to reach "inside" the computer and create. Great editors know that the more brainpower they can put toward their edit session (not edit system), the better their show turns out.

Practice your scales. Don't skimp on learning Final Cut Pro's interface—after all, you paid good money for a Baby Grand, so learn to play it well.

Get Dynamic with Interfaces

One of the coolest new features of Final Cut Pro 4 is the dynamic resizing of the interface. You can now quickly adjust the size of windows using dynamic resizing. Clicking between two windows or at the intersection of multiple windows allows you to drag and resize all windows. You no longer have to resize one window at a time.

Need more space in the timeline? Just grab the top edge, and pull upward. Want to see more in the viewer? Grab the edge, and pull to the right. It's simple to quickly change the size of a window and view exactly what you need.

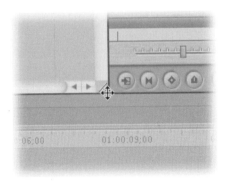
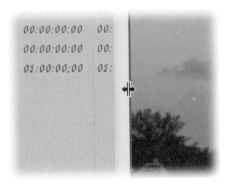

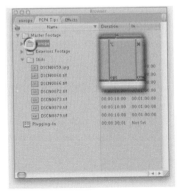

Better Bins

Want to Open a Bin, without eating up more window space. You can hold down the Option key and double-click a bin's icon to open it as a tab in its parent's window. This helps keep your interface lean and clean.

Make It Big

Depending on your work style, you may like to make your tracks taller or shorter. Tall tracks are great when you are looking at your audio waveforms. Shorter tracks are helpful when you're trying to composite multiple layers. Previous versions of Final Cut shipped with four preset track heights. But now you can change them individually.

Click on the thin gray line between tracks and grab. You can now drag and size the height of each track individually.

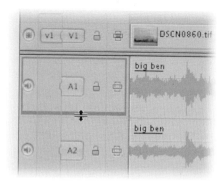

Make It Big (Part 2)

Hold down the Option key and you can size all of your video *or* audio tracks at once.

Hold down the Shift key, and you can size *all* tracks at once.

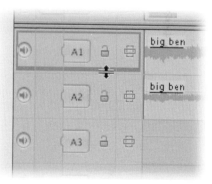

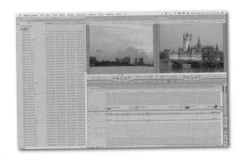

That's the Spot

You've perfectly configured your windows. Every palette is exactly where you want it. The timeline has just enough room and you've got the audio meter exactly where it should be. Now save that window arrangement.

Long-term storage

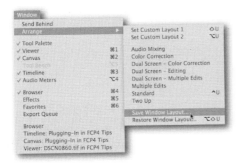

1 Choose Window > Arrange > Save Layout. This setting is stored by default in your Window Layouts folder.

2 Final Cut Pro 4 also adds custom layouts to the bottom of the list with a new keyboard shortcut automatically assigned.

3 Now call up your Button List (Tools > Button List) or Option + J and type the word **window**. Grab the Window Layout button and drag it to a convenient button well.

*** Note that the Custom layout is an alphabetized list. Number your layouts when saving them. Example 1. Effects, 2. Compositing, and so on.)

Short-term storage

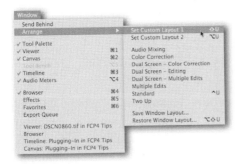

Still testing the layout to make sure you like it? You can save it temporarily in one of two custom positions. Hold down the Option key, and choose Window > Arrange > Set Custom Layout. Now when you return, you will find the Custom Layouts have been set.

Move the Dock

The dock was not designed for use with Final Cut Pro. Seems like its always popping up and getting in the way. In its default position (bottom of the screen) it can eat away valuable monitor space that you could use for your timeline. But like most things in OS X, there's a preference that can be changed.

❶ Go to the Apple menu and choose Dock > Dock Preferences or Contextual-clicking on the separator bar in the Dock.

❷ Tell the system that you want to automatically hide and show the dock. This will put the dock away when it's not in use.

❸ Change the dock's position. Placing the dock on the left or right side of the screen will allow you to have more screen real-estate for your timeline.

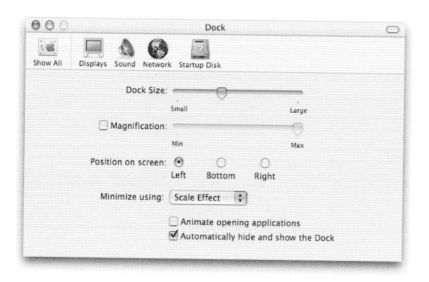

Kill the Dock

If you are tired of the Dock popping up in your way, there are two methods to 'kill it.'

Permanently

❶   Log in as the root user (see Apple Knowledge Base article 106290.)

❷   Access the dock by navigating System > Library > Core Services > Dock.

❸   Move the dock into your applications folder or leave it on the desktop.

❹   You can choose to make it a log in item, and then quit it before running Final Cut Pro.

Temporarily

To temporarily destroy it, follow these steps:

❶   Several programmers have released Dock disabling utilities. Simply visit a website such as VersionTracker.com and type **kill Dock** into the search field.

❷   One such application, killDock, seems stable in our opinion.

❸   A quick visit to VersionTracker will give you several options for Dock utilities.

    In all 'Dock'-less cases the shareware application ASM by Frank Vercruesse is useful for switching between open applications.

Lock Down

Want to preserve a video track? Then lock it. Hold down F4 and then type a track number using the top row of number keys. You can lock tracks V1 – V9. For audio locking, use F5 and a number key. This is a great way to avoid "accidental" edits.

Lock Down II

Need to work on one video track without affecting any others? Hold down the Option key and click on your desired track's lock icon. All other video tracks will be locked. To unlock all tracks, simply hold down Option and click the lock icon again. This trick also works on audio tracks.

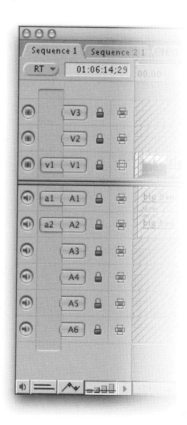

Global Lock Down

Need to lock all your video or audio tracks? Simply press Shift + F4 to lock video tracks or Shift + F5 to lock all audio tracks. Repeat the key combo to unlock all tracks.

Keys to the Locks

If you find yourself needing to lock and unlock tracks often, remember you can customize your keyboard layout. We suggest mapping the toggle track locks to a Function Key combo. For example, try mapping Toggle Track Lock V1-V8 to Option + F1–F8. You can then map Toggle Track A1-A8 to Option + Command + F1–F8. This will significantly speed up your timeline editing ability.

Here or There?

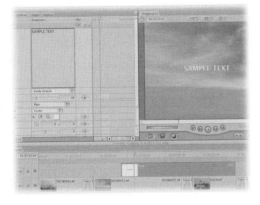

It's important to realize the difference of working with browser clips and timeline clips. This is critical when creating titles. When you generate a title, you should immediately drag it into the timeline and then reload it into the viewer (by double-clicking it in the timeline). That way you can see how your modifications look against the final image. You can do the same with filters. Conversely if you drop a filter on an item in the browser, it's available in all future uses of the clip.

Am I Loaded?

You're working on a clip in the viewer, but you can't remember if you loaded it from your browser or the timeline. Not a problem. Final Cut Pro distinguishes between clips opened from the Browser and clips opened from the Timeline. Clips opened from the Browser have a plain scrubber bar, those loaded from the Timeline have two rows of dots in the scrubber bar, similar to the sprocket holes in a strip of film.

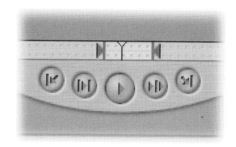

Clean Your Room

Creative people are often messy; it's much more fun to create than it is to clean. While building an effect or tweaking an audio filter, it's not uncommon to tear the Audio, Filters, or Motion tab off to have greater access to controls. But what about when its time to go on to the next challenge? Not to worry…just double click to load the next clip into the viewer. All of your tabs restore themselves into their default position. Now if our desks could only stay so clean.

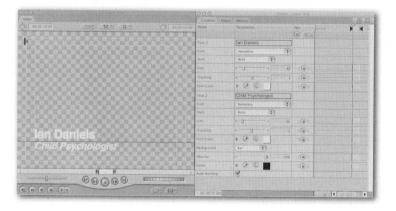

OS X: Child-Proof Windows No More

Miss the ability to roll a window up? The window shade feature of OS9 was a nice way to keep a window open, but out of the way (allowing you to quickly jump into your Finder without having to hide Final Cut Pro or minimize a window.) Until Apple decides to put this feature back, there's a great alternative. WindowShade X from Unsanity.com is a reasonably priced option that allows you to collapse windows. As a bonus, it also can make windows transparent or minimize them in place. Our favorite feature is the ability to disable the Minimize to Dock option. This will prevent you from accidentally banishing a bin or window when you click its title bar.

Time on Your Side

Are you the decisive type? Know exactly what you want? Then this shortcut is for you. It's possible to specify the exact duration for a shot, quickly.

❶ Mark an In point by pressing I in the Viewer.

❷ Press Tab; the duration field is now highlighted.

❸ Type in the desired duration, but omit any colons or semicolons (for example, type **315** for a duration of 3:15)

❹ Press Enter. The new Out point is marked.

What's Your Destination?

Need to define on which track your video edit will occur? Then you need to set its destination. Hold down F6 and then type a track number using the top row of number keys. You can set tracks V1–V9. For setting an audio's destination, use F7 to patch A1 and F8 to patch A2. If you want to switch tracks again, you will need to press the F key again. Laptop users will need to use the fn + the F key to get the same results.

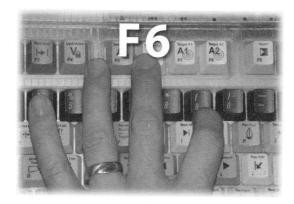

Gear Down

When using filters, you'll often want to make 'fine' adjustments. You can always switch to numeric entry, but most users find the graphic interfaces more intuitive. Simply hold down the Command key to "gear down." The sliders or control points will move much more slowly. This tip works in several places, including audio.

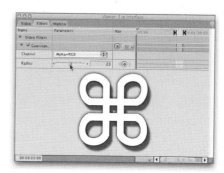

ON THE SPOT

CHAPTER 2

Setting Up for Success
User Settings for Best Performance

Preferences, preferences, preferences. These are the settings that turn an off-the-lot car into a supercharged racing machine. User settings not only make Final Cut Pro work better and faster, they make it work better and faster for you. They tune the engine to your style of driving.

One of the beauties of Final Cut Pro is that it's "plug and play." You can literally edit DV right out of the box. What's even better is how flexible and scalable it is. You can work with DV, SD, HD, film, 24p, internal drives, external drives, PAL, NTSC...the list goes on. But all that flexibility means you need to configure your system. Beyond hardware configuration, there are even more options to set. How do you want Final Cut Pro to modify graphic files? How often should it save a backup copy? What's the default number of audio tracks in a new sequence? You can customize hundreds of settings. This chapter will help you fine-tune your NLE system's performance and ensure less headaches down the road.

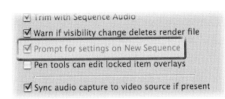

Get It Right from the Start: Using Presets

If you're working with multiple formats and resolutions, this is a critical preference: It's easy to create a new sequence and have it set up improperly for the media you are working on. So, check the "Prompt for settings on New Sequence" checkbox, and Final Cut Pro will ask you to set your sequence settings each time you create a new sequence.

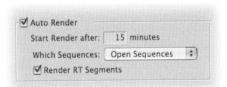

Even Forgetful People Can be Efficient

This new feature is made for long client phone calls, unexpected staff meetings, or alien abductions. Even if you forget to render, Final Cut Pro can automatically render your work for you. Simply check the "Auto Render" box on the General tab of the User Preferences panel. Tell Final Cut Pro how long to wait and which sequences to render. You can also choose whether to render real-time segments—we usually do.

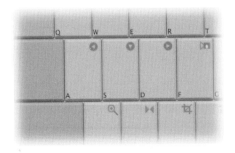

Batting Lefty

J-K-L editing is the most useful shortcut for fast editing. But a lot of lefties find it fatiguing to drive righthanded. Harness Final Cut Pro 4's mappable keyboard. Go to Tools>Keyboard Layout>Customize (Option + H), and unlock your keyboard. Now drag the J, K, and L keys to A, S, and D, respectively. While you're there, set W and E to be In and Out, respectively, and then edit away.

Foreshadowing: Using Pre-roll

We usually find that Final Cut Pro shows too much Preview Pre-Roll. When trimming on the fly or reviewing an edit point, pre-roll allows you to review what happens before an edit. The default preference is 5:00. However, we usually find that two or three seconds is adequate. And, hey, every second counts when trying to meet a deadline.

A "Dupious" Achievement

Dupe detection has its origins in film editing. If you repeat a shot, you need to duplicate that clip because the physical film can't be in two places at once. Dupe detection is designed to warn film editors of this problem.

Video editors can benefit, as well. Think of this as a "dummy" switch. When enabled, dupe detection alerts you if you've used a particular shot already in your timeline. This can be useful when cutting B-Roll into a long-format show.

ToolTips Give Psychic Powers

Want to quickly learn the name and shortcuts for your tools? That's why ToolTips are there. Just hover over an unknown button, and you'll often discover its name and keyboard shortcut. If this isn't working, check the "Show ToolTips" box on the General tab of the User Preferences panel.

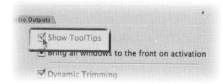

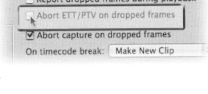

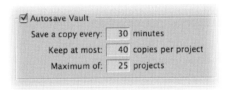

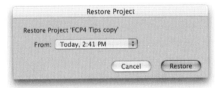

How to Miss FedEx

You're rushing to get a rough cut out to the client for review purposes. Maybe you've rendered everything or you've taken advantage of Final Cut Pro 4's ability to output frames via FireWire without rendering. Then, 25 minutes into your 30-minute program, the Print to Video command aborts because of a dropped frame.

Yes, dropped frames are bad. But missed deadlines are worse. Disable the "Abort ETT/PTV on dropped frames" checkbox on the General tab of the User Preferences panel when you're making a rushed output on a deadline. This will keep the layout from being aborted. Restore the dropped tape option when making archival masters of your program.

CYA

Ever have a project go bad? A file get corrupted? Maybe the system crashed (OS X never crashes...it just has an undocumented close feature). Worse, you come back from lunch, and the client is standing over your editing system. "I just pushed a few buttons, really!"

It's okay if the Autosave Vault feature is turned on. This great feature will back up your project automatically. You tell it how often to save, how many versions to save, and how many projects total can be archived. This is a great way to cover yourself against unexpected events.

If things ever go wrong, simply choose File>Restore Project. This way you can quickly access time-stamped versions of your project. After restoring a project, immediately select the Save Project As command and revert to the original name. Otherwise, the Autosave Vault feature will start building a new project folder for the project with a name such as FCP4 Tips_08_12_03_0241.

Use this the next time a producer pulls a 180-degree turn on you and wants to go back three hours in time.

You Do, He Do, She Do, Undo

If you've got RAM, you might as well use it. Final Cut Pro supports up to 99 levels of undo. Your safety net just got bigger. But remember, more undos will cut into your performance, so find a good balance that works for you and your machine.

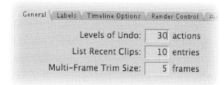

Hear More in Real-Time

Switching your audio playback quality to the Low setting will allow you more channels of real-time audio. Don't worry; on a Print to Video or Edit to Tape command, Final Cut Pro will automatically switch to maximum quality.

In a Vacuum

It's essential to get your Trim preferences set correctly. Otherwise, you might as well wear earmuffs and pull a hat over your eyes. In the User Preferences panel, make sure the following settings are checked:

- **Dynamic Trimming:** This allows you to use your J-K-L keys for trimming in the Trim Edit window. You can roll the edit point back and forth.

- **Trim with Sequence Audio** If you can't hear it, you can't trim it.

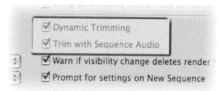

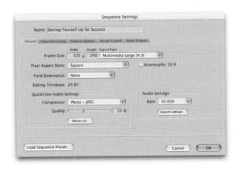

Seeing Red

If you're getting red bars across all your footage as soon as you add to the timeline, you're probably not configured correctly. It's likely that the last project you worked on used a different configuration (such as Widescreen or Offline RT). Check your sequence's settings (Command + 0 (zero)).

Sequence Settings

There are a few places to change sequence settings. The important detail to remember is which settings you want to change.

Selecting Final Cut Pro>User Preferences and going to the Timeline Options tab allows you to modify all future sequences.

Selecting Sequence>Settings (Command + 0) or selecting the Timeline submenu allows you to modify the current sequence only. You must have the Canvas or Timeline selected for this command to work.

Avoiding the Capture Blues

Nothing is more frustrating then having a clip abort capture, especially if that clip is a long performance piece that you're loading and it bails after only 16 minutes. Be sure to select Make New Clip from the On timecode break setting.

More Than Meets the Eye: Inside the Package

Warning: Throw out the wrong things, and you can really mess up your applications.

In OS X nearly every native application is really a folder containing all the resources it needs to operate. But every time you click that "folder," the application launches. The trick is, go to the applications folder and Control + click the Final Cut Pro icon. You'll see a pull-down menu. Click the Show Package Contents command.   Inside you'll see a Contents folder—welcome to Pandora's box.

Warning: throw out the wrong things and you can really mess up your applications

When You Don't Want Your PALs Around
(or NTSCs If You're from the Other Side of the Pond)

Warning: Deleting your Final Cut Pro 4 preferences deletes all sorts of stuff. You'll lose your recent files, favorites, custom effects, motions, and transitions. See the "Master Backup project" tip in Chapter 12 to preserve some of your favorites and customizations in advance.

So you only work in NTSC (you may substitute PAL throughout) and want to rid your Audio/Video Settings folder of those options? Here's the trick : You need to remove these presets in the package located inside the Contents folder by drilling down this path: Resources > English.lproj > Final Cut Pro Settings > Hardware Settings. You'll see four presets: two NTSC and two PAL. Now delete the ones you don't want.

Now comes the second part: You need to delete and rebuild the user settings in your user preferences folder. This is located in the Final Cut Pro user data folder in your user settings. Just search for Final Cut Pro 4.0 Preferences, and delete. The next time you start Final Cut Pro 4, all your PALs will be gone.

Where Are My Help Docs?

On the Final Cut Pro 4 install disk, there's a Documents folder. It contains PDFs of the manuals for SoundTrack, LiveType, Cinema Tools, and Compressor. Where are the PDFs for Final Cut Pro? Well, you may have discovered you can find them in the Help pull-down menu when in Final Cut Pro. But how would you like a PDF copy you can click to open?

Here's how to find them: Open the package for Final Cut Pro. Inside the Contents folder, drill down this path: Resources > English.lproj > Final Cut Pro Help > and Voila! You'll find all five Final Cut Pro 4 PDFs.

Next, Option + drag them to your desktop to make a copy of the files. (If you just drag them, you won't have access to them in the Help pull-down menu.)

Streamline Your Presets

Now let's say you want to rid yourself of all those other pesky settings you never use, such as OfflineRT NTSC (Photo JPEG) – 23.98. Drill down to <system drive> >Library>Application Support>Final Cut Pro System Support>Custom Settings. Now, duplicate the Custom Settings folder, and rename it **Custom Settings Backup**. Open the original Custom Settings folder, and throw away any settings you don't want to clutter your settings. Once again, you need to delete and rebuild your user preferences for these changes to take effect.

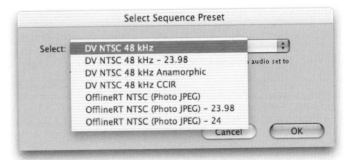

How to Kill a Hard Drive

The best way to kill a drive is to fill it up so much that it essentially locks up. Final Cut Pro seems to have a death wish when it comes to hard drives. Call up your system settings, and check the "Minimum Allowable Free Space on Scratch Disks" field.

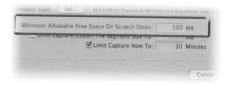

You'll notice that the default setting is that your scratch disks will fill up to within 10MB before being seen as full. This is like driving in the desert with less than a quarter-gallon of gas. Be sure to change this number to 500MB or 5 percent of a drive's capacity, whichever number is bigger. This way you'll have room for other files such as graphics or music associated with a project.

Danger...Danger (Aww Shut Up)

In the past, Final Cut Pro warned you when a device wasn't present—the thought being you might not actually notice that someone came in and walked off with your camera or deck. Fortunately, the engineers decided that after four versions, we could have a choice.

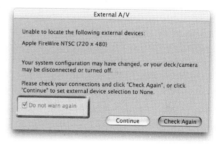

If you're tired of clicking OK every time you launch Final Cut Pro on your laptop, check the "Do not warn again" box the first time you're presented with the warning dialog box. If you ever change your mind, call up your Audio/Video Settings and go to the A/V Devices tab to re-enable the warning.

ON THE SPOT

CHAPTER 3

Notching It Up
Taking Effects to the Next Level

Is this the chapter you turned to first? Probably…it's the one we would've turned to first. As an editor, you want to dazzle your clients with effects and make your shows sparkle. You want to be the slickest editor on the block, with the biggest bag of tricks. No problem, you supply the bag…we'll supply the tricks. However, be prepared to push yourself. Good effects take more than drag and drop. They take time to learn and build. The more you use them, the faster you'll be able to create them and the further you'll go.

In this chapter, we've pulled together some of the top effects that our clients love such as a film-look treatment and a blown-out treatment. More important, though, we'll teach you how the effect interface works. You'll learn techniques that increase your speed when building effects. You'll also learn strategies for faster renders and improved control. Go grab an espresso, a Red Bull, or Jolt cola; fasten your seatbelt; and get ready to notch it up!

Auto Render

We love this feature...but use it wisely. In the user preferences file, there's a checkbox to have Final Cut Pro automatically render your sequences after a certain amount of idle time. (You can set this anywhere from 1 to 120 minutes.) You can have it render all open sequences, the current sequence, or all open sequences except for the current sequence.

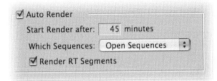

So what does this mean to you? Well, if you wander away for a cup or coffee and get yanked into a meeting (or locked in a closet), your show could be rendered upon your return. This is very cool.

However, you may not always want this to happen. Suppose you're just playing around with an effect or composite. If Final Cut Pro keeps rendering every time you're idle, your hard drive could fill up with out-of-date render files pretty quickly. So perhaps you'll want to set your preferences to auto-render all the open sequences except for the current one just to be safe.

This is a cool and powerful tool, but like the magic wand in the Sorcerer's Apprentice, you could be up to your neck in water (or render files) if you aren't careful.

Freeze Frame: Setting Duration of Stills

The Still/Freeze Duration preference has been around since version 1, but a lot of folks don't use it to its full advantage. Whenever you create a freeze of an image or drag in a still such as a PICT, TIFF, PSD, or JPEG file, the resulting clip is your default still/freeze duration. This, by the way, is factory set at 10 seconds (with total handles of 1:50 seconds, making the clip really two minutes long).

Suppose you're creating a slide show to music. Instead of leaving the default at 10 seconds, set it to five. This way you won't have to readjust every clip you import.

Now suppose you're doing an animation. You could change the duration to one frame! Drag it into your timeline, and you've just edited an animated sequence. (You can also use QuickTime to merge a sequence of PICT files into a QuickTime movie.)

The secret is Final Cut Pro will assign whatever the current default duration is to your images at the moment they're brought into the browser. So feel free to change this throughout your project to meet your immediate needs.

Effects Tip – Moving Tab

A lot of folks still don't realize they can rip tabs off their canvas window. This is helpful if you've loaded a clip from the browser or have a generator loaded. So when you're editing effects, pull the Video tab off and place it next to the Filters tab. Now as you make changes, you don't need to toggle back and forth between tabs to see how your video is affected.

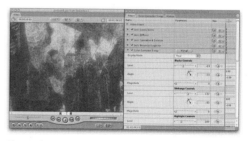

Photo credit James Ball

When RT Extreme Is Not Enough

Ever want to preview an effect without rendering? Sure, you say, that's why there's RT Extreme. The number of effects, the data rate of the video files, and the speed of your machine drive real-time preview. Things can get so demanding that your computer may not be able to keep up...then what?

The solution is to force Final Cut Pro to Play Every Frame. To do this, simply press Option + P to invoke a non-real-time preview. You can now view every frame (at less than 1x speed) without dropping any frames.

Big Effects: More Room to Keyframe

On a one-monitor system or laptop? Trying to keyframe filters in the viewer is tough. There's not nearly enough space to view effect parameters and keyframes. You can scroll back and forth all day long and drag windows constantly.

The solution is simple. Grab the Filters tab, and dock it with the Timeline. You'll now have plenty of room to modify the effect. When you load a new clip, the Filters tab "redocks" itself to the canvas. Although the tearing of tabs is repetitive, the extra room will come in handy when keyframing advanced effects.

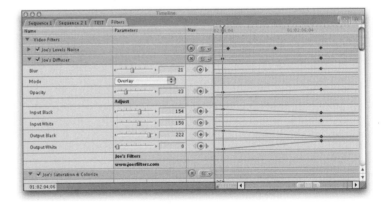

Go Outside and Play: Using External Editors

Want even more filters and effects? No problem, use a companion program. Depending on your needs (and price range), there are several excellent programs for processing your video. Although we love our Final Cut Pro systems, we're "equal opportunity" when it comes to getting the job done. Depending on the filters we need to access, we may send a clip to QuickTime Pro or Adobe After Effects.

Why leave Final Cut Pro? Well, there are several filters and effects available from different vendors. There are some great (and very affordable) filters for QuickTime Pro, for instance. There are also filters built into After Effects and available from third-party companies that don't work in Final Cut Pro.

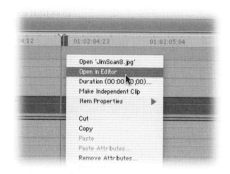

To make a smooth transition between applications is an easy process. All you need to do is tell Final Cut Pro which application to use to edit QuickTime files. Go to Final Cut Pro> System Settings, and then click the Extern Editors tab. You can set an outside application to process video files. Now just Control + click a file in your timeline, and choose Open in Editor.

Apply any filters or effects to your clip. Unlike Adobe Photoshop files, you cannot just save your changes. Now you must render or export the file back out of the editor. Once the effect is applied, the new video clip can be edited back into your show.

A/B Effect

Need to compare what a clip looks like with and without filters? Clients always seem to ask this question, so you might as well know. You might think it's easy—just turn all the checkboxes off next to each filter name, right? But it wouldn't be Final Cut Pro 4 if there weren't a better way.

One of the new items in the tool bench is a Frame Viewer (Option + 7). This tool has several purposes (especially for color correction). But when building effects, it's very useful. Follow these steps:

1 Place the cursor over the clip you want to use. You may want to switch to the Color Correction workspace. When you do, you'll notice that the frame viewer is docked with the scopes in the upper-right corner.

2 At the bottom of the Frame Viewer, choose what you'd like to see; in this case, that's the current frame and the current frame without filters.

3 Select a V-Split or H-Split to view both states of the clip.

You can grab the blue or green squares and customize your split.

Stealing Effects

Thanks to Final Cut Pro's improved media management, you can now steal rendered effects from one sequence and place them in another. Perhaps you have a clip that has had several image effects applied to it; you can copy this to your Clipboard and paste it into another sequence. As long as you don't composite anything on top of it, your render files should stick. Any transitions will just need the overlapping handles rendered.

Effects Mode

Avid editors often complain that Final Cut Pro lacks an Effects mode. "Why must I double-click a clip every time to see its controls?" Well, we agree all that extra clicking can get tiresome. Good news: So does Apple!

Follow these steps to create an Effects mode:

❶ In the middle of your Canvas is the Playhead Sync menu. Simply pick Open.

❷ In the Viewer, choose the Filters tab.

Now every time you pause on a clip, the effect controls will pop open. Don't worry–Final Cut Pro will not try to open tabs when you're playing your sequence, only when paused.

My Effects are Broken

Every time we speak, someone asks us about why sometimes his or her effects don't work. Upon further propping, we discover they keep getting a black screen on unrendered effects. The answer the Caps Lock key.

If you're using intensive effects, you sometimes want to disable them for faster navigation within the timeline. This can also be helpful if you don't want to wait for screen redraw while tweaking an effect. Just press the Caps Lock key. All non-RT effects are disabled.

My Caps Lock Key is Broken

For those in the know, the previous tip on the Caps Lock key is somewhat universal. In Adobe Photoshop it disables brush previews; in Adobe After Effects it disables screen redraw. So why when you press it in Final Cut Pro does it no longer work?

In Final Cut Pro 4, only clips that require rendering for playback (indicated by a red bar) are disabled. If you've turned on the Unlimited RT feature, those clips that aren't true real-time will still play back in a limited fashion. You may want to switch to Safe RT mode using the RT pop-up menu in the timeline.

Gotta Good Board?

Final Cut Pro 4 has an Effect Handling tab in the System Settings window. This is where you can specify how real-time effects are handled for different real-time-capable codecs. Your board or accelerator must be compatible and capable of handling the effects. Be sure to see the owner's manual or website of your accelerator to properly calibrate these settings.

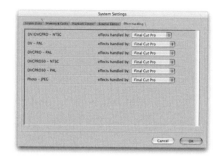

Steal from Yourself

It's okay to save time by lifting keyframes or parameters from one clip and pasting them to another. We use this all the time while editing audio or creating title effects. The simple truth is this is one of the biggest time savers out there.

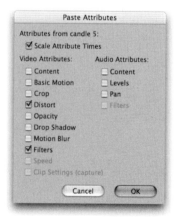

❶ Select a clip that has the properties you want to access with the Select tool.

❷ Contextual click the clip, and choose Copy.

❸ Select the target clip, and contextual click it.

❹ Choose Paste Attributes, and select the desired parameters from the pop-up dialog box.

Needs Render	
Rendered Proxy	
Proxy	⌥⌘P
Preview	⌃R
Full	
Unlimited	
For Playback	
Item Level	
Mixdown	⌥⌘R

Like a Kid in a Candy Store...

Because there are now so many versions of "real-time" in Final Cut Pro 4, several colors became necessary to mark them in the timeline. The old colors made sense: Green = Go, Red = Stop. But now, even we have to stop and think.

Here's a short guide to what all those colors mean:

Dark Gray	No rendering needed
Steel Gray	Already been rendered.
Dark Green	Real-time effect that can be output to video at full quality without rendering. Green Will play back in the computer in real-time. However, when going out over FireWire or qualified card, the effect will play at a lower quality.
Yellow	The effect you see is an approximation. Final Cut Pro may revert to default angles for transitions or may remove soft edges. The effect plays, but not all parameters are displayed while the effect is in motion.
Dark Yellow	The effect has been rendered at a lower frame rate or quality setting than the current sequence settings. Render files are now preserved after switching resolutions.
Orange	The effect has exceeded your machine's real-time ability. However these effects are partially enabled because of Unlimited RT being chosen. likely to drop frames on orange clips, but this is a useful way to preview without rendering.
Blue	You've installed unsupported real-time enabler files. These blue bars indicate areas of your timeline that may drop frames if not rendered. Blue bars are rare and may be an indication that a hardware device is no longer installed or is malfunctioning because the drivers are trying to process real-time effects but can't access the required power.
Red	You broke it! The RT ability of your machine has been exceeded. The red bar may come sooner than you'd like on older machines, but newer processors have shown significant ability to playback with Unlimited RT turned on.

RT to the Max

RT Extreme is one of the biggest additions to Final Cut Pro 4. You not only get more layers of real-time effects, but you get real-time out to your NTSC monitor. How can you get even more layers of real-time effects? Final Cut Pro looks for the following:

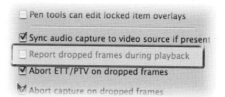

❶ The faster the better. A brand-spanking-new dual-processor G5 is going to give you way more real-time functionality than your "ancient" G4 500. The more random access memory (RAM), the better. And every school kid knows the faster your bus is, the better off you are–but that's system bus, not school bus.

❷ Make sure the Unlimited RT feature is turned on and your playback quality is set to Low. You'll want to tell your system to ignore dropped frames (unless you enjoy clicking the OK button).

❸ Turn off your external monitor if you're not using it (by selecting View>External Video>Off). External monitoring can sap a layer or two from your real-time. (If you edit in Offline RT mode, you get even more layers.)

Remember, when you're pushing the limit of RT...yreal-time, you may drop a frame or two. That's okay–you're building and designing the show, so you should always render before you output to a master tape.

Precision Preview

Wouldn't it be nice to preview your complex effects without actually rendering to disk? It's a pain getting your hard drive all cluttered with extra render files that eat up drive space. Well, you have a solution; you can render to RAM.

The QuickView is a great way to view your sequence outside of the Canvas window. It caches frames into RAM as you play it:

❶ The QuickView creates no render files, which is good for media management.

❷ If you preview an effect and like it, you'll still have to render before you can do finally output. QuickView is for previewing only.

❸ You can choose Full, Half, or Quarter as your viewing resolution. Lower quality will speed up previews but may impact certain effects that contain mattes or fine edges.

❹ Be sure you have specified which video to cache:

- Auto chooses the Viewer or the Canvas, whichever is active.
- Viewer or Canvas caches from the selected window.

❺ None disables preview (we know…silly choice).

❻ When finished, be sure to close the QuickView window and free up your RAM.

❼ If you misplace the QuickView window, select Window> Tool Bench. Otherwise, you'll open a second (or third…) QuickView window.

How Much Is That Preview in the Window?

When using QuickView, you must specify how much area to preview. Only preview what you need because the rest is just wasted time. There are four ways to set a preview duration:

❶ **Using both In and Out points:** Set a specific range in your timeline for QuickView to use.

❷ **Using an In point:** QuickView will preview the number of seconds specified with range slider, beginning at the In point.

❸ **Using an Out point:** QuickView will preview the number of seconds specified with range slider, ending at the Out point.

❹ **Not setting any marks:** QuickView will cache the duration set with the range slider. The preview will be split in half using the playhead, half occurring before and half after.

Pull Back to See More

Compositing or setting up an animation path? You'll want to choose Fit All from the canvas's View menu. This allows you to see the bounding boxes of all elements, even those dragged partially off the screen.

"Instant" Backgrounds

Need a modern-looking moving background? No problem—simply process a video clip into a soft-moving texture. Here's one recipe that couldn't be easier to follow:

1 Select your clip of video. Choose a clip that contains some of the colors you'd like to use; close-ups or soft shots work best.

2 Apply the Wind Blur filter by choosing Effects> Video Filters> Blur> Wind Blur.

3 Set the angle to taste. Try 90 degrees or –90 degrees for starters.

4 Leave the radius at 100, but turn the Steps control to five or higher.

5 Now you need to apply the same effect again. The best way is to Copy and Paste. Highlight the effect in the Viewer's Filters tab and press Command + C. Then press Command + V to paste the effect again.

6 Apply the effect five or more times.

7 Apply a Gaussian Blur filter, and set the blur to only the RGB Channels. Turn the radius up to taste.

8 Render. It'll take a while but no longer than any motion graphics application.

9 Mark an In and Out point, and choose File> Export> QuickTime Movie. Make this self-contained and re-import it into your project. This way you won't have to re-render it again.

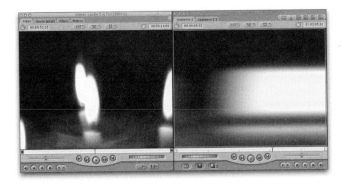

Digital Concealer

Little too much detail in your skin tones? If the subject's pores are just jumping off the screen, you can use this effect to soften skin. This can be useful when polishing a shot or as a precursor to additional effects work.

❶ Select the clip to be processed.

❷ Apply the Channel Blur filter by selecting Effects> Video Filters> Channel> Channel Blur. This effect allows you to blur a specific channel of information.

❸ Be sure to view this effect in High Quality mode to make the best judgment. The best way to do this is to view the clip while paused.

❹ By default, a two-pixel blur is applied to all channels. Adjust the blur on individual channels to reduce noise. For skin tones, you'll usually blur the blue or green channels. Be sure to reduce any blur on the red channel.

Photo credit James Ball

CGM Double Border

CGM Double Border was one of our favorite filters that shipped with Final Cut Pro 3. If you had it installed when you upgraded, it moved to your Final Cut Pro 4 plug-ins folder. If not, simply pull out your Final Cut Pro 3 disc and manually install the plug-in.

Here's why we think it's so cool:

❶ With the Apple Border filter, you can't crop or the border gets cut off.

❷ With the CGM filter, you can adjust how much of the image you see, adjust how thick the border is, and crop on the fly. You can even keyframe all these effects.

❸ The effect works in real-time in version 4.

❹ To position the picture in picture (PIP), just switch over to the wireframe view.

Note: We love using this filter when creating looping DVD menus. It's great for PIP effects and buttons.

f CGM Double Border

Video Wall

This is pretty fun. Shoot your interview green screen, and get ready to chroma key. To build a video wall as a backdrop, follow these steps:

1 Pick the shot you want behind your speaker.

2 Drop on a Bevel filter (Effects> Video Filters> Border> Bevel). Adjust to taste.

3 Next, add a replicate filter and set it to 3x3. The scene should start to look like a video wall.

Here's the trick: Create a sense of depth by adding a Gaussian Blur filter to the wall effect. Experiment with the radius of the blur to defocus the background. Now when you key it into the background, it looks as if your cameraperson lit it perfectly for a shallow depth of field.

Photo credit Hemera Photo Objects

Video Wall 2

Want to take the effect even further (and your render times higher?)? Apply the effects in the following order:

1 Select a shot.

2 Slightly desaturate the shot using the Desaturate video filter.

3 Apply a Basic Border set to 50. Set the color to black or dark gray.

4 Apply a Bevel to 80. Use a small width (such as 3), and lower the opacity.

5 Apply a Lens Flare filter. Use a size of 1 and a brightness of 1. Position the flare in a corner to add a sense of direction.

6 Apply the replicate filter and set it to 3x3, 4x4, and so on to match your needs.

Film Look: Soft Bloom

On several occasions, there has been a crazy notion passed around that Digital Video signals can be somehow manipulated (mangled?) into the look of a film-look. Although we don't subscribe to this belief, it's quite possible to achieve a nicer look for your flat video images.

The trait that people often are trying to achieve with their "film-look" filters or recipes is an increase in saturation (intensity of color). You can easily accomplish this look in Final Cut Pro using built-in filters and features. Follow these steps:

❶ Select the clip (with the arrow tool) you'd like to process using the film look.

❷ Drag straight up while holding down the Option key. This clones the shot.

❸ With the clone highlighted, apply a Gaussian Blur effect. Crank the filter up between a radius of 15 and 90 pixels. Don't worry if it looks awful.

❹ Control + click the clip in your timeline, and try different composite modes such as Overlay, Soft Light, or Multiply. In fact, you may want to try all of the different modes to see which one you like. Depending on your source, you may want to use different modes.

❺ Adjust the opacity of the top clip to taste.

❻ If you need to color correct the shot, nest it first.

Film Look: Blown-Out

So you want to create a blown-out look and still keep you clip broadcast legal?

Here's a quick way to do it:

❶ Open the Color Correction window arrangement so that you can see your scopes.

❷ Take your clip, and duplicate it on the track above (by pressing Shift + Option and dragging).

❸ Now, on the upper clip, add a Gaussian Blur filter with a radius of about 20.

❹ Pull the opacity of this layer down to about 35 percent. (These numbers will vary depending on your image.)

❺ Now drop on a three-way color corrector. Use it as a proc amp to reduce the luminance of the whites circle and raise the luminance of the midtones.

❻ Now the fun begins. Control + click the upper clip, and change the composite layer to Add. You'll see that your whites are starting to get blown out but that you've exceeded broadcast safe on your overall luminance levels. Fear not, the next step contains the trick.

❼ Use the Broadcast Safe filter to bring everything into a legal zone. But it won't work by dropping it onto just one or both clips; you must nest the two clips together before you drop the Broadcast Safe filter. Select both clips, and press Option + C to collapse the two tracks into a nest. Ah ha…a blown-out image that still caps at 100 IRE.

Chroma Key is Not Just For Weather

Creating a chroma key in Final Cut Pro is pretty easy. The trick is to use a new filter under the Key drop-down called Color Smoothing – 4:1:1 (for DV-25) or Color Smoothing – 4:2:2: (for DVCPRO-50 and 8-bit and 10-bit uncompressed clips). Remember, use this filter before using the Chroma Keyer filter.

Now, drop the Chroma Keyer filter onto your shot, and click the dropper tool to sample the color you want to key out. You can press Shift + click with the dropper to select an even wider range of colors. We often zoom the image 200–400 percent so that we can sample all the pixels. You should also tweak the edge thin and softness sliders, too, which gives you a cleaner key. (Remember, with these sliders, a little goes a long way.)

Blue and Green Screen
Chroma Keyer
Color Key
Color Smoothing – 4:1:1
Color Smoothing – 4:2:2
Difference Matte
Luma Key
Spill Suppressor – Blue
Spill Suppressor – Green

Stay on Target

Zoomed all the way into an effect while editing a motion path? Up close working on a matte effect such as a chroma key? You can see the effect play, in its entirety, without having to zoom out.

❶ Mark an In and an Out point on the area you'd like to preview.

❷ Call up the QuickView window by pressing Option + 8.

❸ Set the resolution of the effect and click Play. The first time through, the effect is building (and not playing in real-time). Subsequently, the effect will loop and play back in real-time.

Note: The duration you can preview is determined by the resolution, amount of effects, and total amount of RAM available.

ON THE SPOT

A Cut Above
Building Better Transitions

"Oh, a star wipe transition…pretty!" If you hear this from your client, run away as fast as you can. We've found one good use for this transition in the past 20 years, and that was marginal. However, good transition skills can really impress your clients.

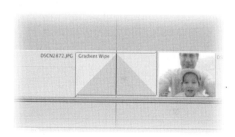

This chapter goes miles beyond "If you can't solve it, dissolve it." We'll teach you customizable effects such as a gradient wipe as well as custom-built transitions available nowhere else. We'll explain when to cut and when not to cut. We'll even teach you the "secret of the wells" (hmmm…sounds like an adventure movie). Following the techniques in this chapter will put you on the fast track to a better-looking show.

Just one word of warning: If you're the type of person who drags their shots to the timeline, you'll have problems with transitions. When you load a shot into the viewer, you can set In and Out points that include handles (extra frames beyond your marks). These handles become the overlap where the transition occurs. Remember: No handle, no transition.

Gradient Wipe

Photo credit Time Image: http://www.timeimage.com/

The gradient wipe is the most useful transition inside Final Cut Pro. Don't be turned off by how the effect looks on its own; without an image dropped in the well, it's useless. The effect creates a transition between two clips by using a luminance map. The transition will occur between the darkest and lightest areas in the map. Why is this so cool? You can create as many transitions as you like using graphic files. Make your own or download away. If you have any previous version of Final Cut Pro, look in the Extras folder; you'll find some really cool free samples to get you started.

What's My Wipe?

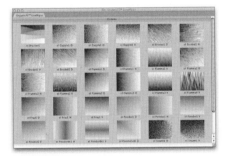

If you want some idea of what your gradient wipe will look like, change your view. By looking at a Gradients icon, you can "see" the shape and direction of the wipe. Simply contextual-click, and choose the View as Large Icons command. By default, the wipe will travel from the darkest areas to the lightest. Remember, you can change the direction of the wipe by clicking the Invert button within the transition controls.

Need Gradients?

Need some inspiration on making gradients for use in transitions? Not sure where to begin? Don't have time to make your own? Visit the following websites for free gradient patterns you can use:

> http://www.fcp4.com
> http://www.autofx.com
> http://www.thepluginsite.com
> http://www.pixelan.com
> http://www.finalcutprohelp.com

Filters As Transitions

You can use any filter as a transition. You just need to combine it with a segment edit and layer the two clips. Throughout this chapter we'll refer to this as a Layered Transition Stack (LTS).

❶ Place the outgoing clip above the second clip in your timeline.

❷ Adjust the edit points so the two tracks have at least 20 frames of overlap.

❸ With your blade tool or (better yet) the Add Edit command, create segments that are precisely overlapped.

❹ Apply a filter to one or both tracks, and experiment with the effect parameters (we'll show you more examples in the next few pages).

❺ Use opacity keyframes on the top track, or a cross-fade on both tracks, to create a smooth transition between clips.

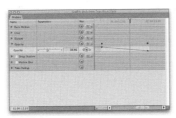

Power Blur #1

This creates a nice transition between two clips. It's particular effective to signify a major transition in time or space and can help if the handles of your clips are very short.

❶   Overlap the two tracks with a Layered Transition Stack (LTS).

❷   Apply a Gaussian Blur filter to the top track.

❸   Keyframe the track to start with a radius of 0.

❹   Apply a second keyframe at the end of the track with a radius of 50 or higher.

❺   Apply a fade to the track by keyframing the opacity.

Optionally, apply the blur in reverse to the lower track as well and make the opacity ramp up quickly. You'll get a dissolve from one blur to another before the incoming shot is revealed, thus creating a more complex transition.

Power Blur # 2

When a simple blur transition begins to look stock to you, take it one step further.

❶   Overlap the two tracks with a LTS.

❷   Apply a Gaussian Blur filter to the top track.

❸   Keyframe the track to start with a radius of 0.

❹   Apply a second keyframe at the end of the track with a radius of 25 or higher.

❺   Add a gradient wipe at the end of the outgoing clip. Experiment—drop different gradient patterns in the well in the Filters tab. Also adjust the softness settings until you get a nice "melting" effect.

Sands of Time

You can use this effect to create a pixel storm–style transition. This effect works best if the transition lasts between two and five seconds.

❶ Overlap the two tracks with a LTS.

❷ Apply a Diffuse filter to the top track (by selecting Effects>Video Filters>Stylize>Diffuse).

❸ Keyframe the track to start with a radius of 0, and set an angle keyframe to 0 degrees.

❹ Apply a second keyframe at the end of the track with a radius of 100. Keyframe the angle to be +180 degrees.

❺ Set the Direction to Non-Directional or Bi-Directional depending on your footage.

❻ Apply a fade to the track by keyframing the opacity.

Optionally, you can apply the effect to both upper and lower tracks to create an alternate transition.

A Page from the Employee Handbook

Don't ask us why, but it seems the Page Peel effect will never die. Clients love using this transition, especially in training videos. But you can improve the effect by dropping a backside onto the wipe.

❶ Import the graphic into your project. This could be a textured file, a video freeze frame, or a piece of corporate wallpaper.

❷ Apply the Page Peel transition to your clip, and adjust the effect to taste.

❸ Drop your new wallpaper into the back well of the transition.

❹ Adjust the radius and highlight controls to further tweak the effect.

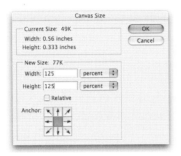

Corporate Wallpaper

Sometimes you want a background for use in a corporate video. We'll create a back page using the client's logo. It's easiest to do this in a graphics program such as Adobe Photoshop:

❶ If working with a square-pixel graphics program, create your document to be 720x534 for DV or 720x540 for SD if you're working with NTSC footage. PAL users should use 768x576. Work in the RGB color space.

❷ Now open your client's logo in a separate document.

❸ Size the logo to be approximately 100 pixels high, and preserve the original aspect ratio for the width.

❹ If the logo is on a locked background layer, float it by Option + clicking on the layer's name.

❺ Press D to load the default colors.

❻ Enlarge the canvas, by choosing Image>Canvas Size. Make the canvas 125 percent of its original size.

❼ Place a new layer behind the logo, and fill it with a complementary color or a secondary color from the approved corporate palette.

❽ Select All by pressing Command + A.

❾ Define the logo as a pattern by selecting Edit>Define Pattern.

❿ Switch back to your square pixel-sized document.

⓫ In the layer's palette, click the circular icon to create a new fill layer. Choose pattern adjustment layer. The last defined pattern (your client's logo) should be available.

⓬ You can click within the window with the move tool to reposition the pattern.

⓭ Flatten the image when you're satisfied with it by pressing Command + E.

⓮ Resize your graphic to the appropriate non-square pixel size, 720x480 for NTSC DV, 720x486 for NTSC SD, 720x576 for PAL, and so on.

⑮ Because it's a back page, you have to flop the image; otherwise, the logo will appear backward when you use it as the backside to an effect. Choose Image>Rotate Canvas>Flip Horizontal.

⑯ Save the graphic as a PICT file with no alpha channel.

Fade Through

Performing a luminance key is a useful way to drop the darkest or lightest elements from a shot. Also, adding keyframes to a luminance key can create a nice transition effect.

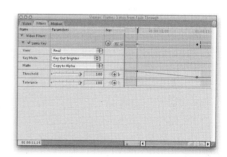

❶ Overlap the two tracks with a LTS.

❷ Apply a Luma Key filter to the top track (by selecting Effects>Video Filters>Key>Luma Key).

❸ To create a light to dark transition, set the effect to Key Out Brighter.

❹ Set the tolerance to 100 to soften the effect.

❺ Apply a threshold keyframe set to +100 at the start of the transition stack.

❻ Apply a second threshold keyframe set to −100 at the end of the transition stack.

Optionally, you can swap the direction of the transition by setting the Luma Key filter to Key Out Darker. Start the effect with a keyframe set to −100 and end with +100.

Retro is Not Always Cool

Most transitions have hard edges. That looks bad enough. Avoid the temptation to add a colored border, or you'll really be traveling back to the days of clunky tapes that were heavier than a 12-inch PowerBook. Instead, try feathering the edges and adjusting the width of the border. In our experience, the client will find the effect far more pleasing.

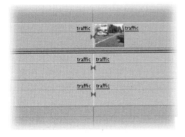

Through Edits

If you've ever bladed a segment in half, you'll see two red triangles facing each other. That's a through edit. (Through edits are turned on in your preferences by default.) This lets you know that even though you see an edit point, there's continuous timecode, so the video will play through uninterrupted.

Un-Blade

Chopped a track to perform a segment effect, such as a multitrack transition? Changed your mind? No big deal...as long as you see the through edit triangles, simply click the edit point to select it. (Make sure you're in the Selection Tool (A)). Then simply press Delete. The edit is now removed, thus joining the two pieces back together.

A Better Cross Zoom

The Cross Zoom transition is a standard transition that pushes the outgoing shot toward the viewer and then snaps back with the incoming shot. The default settings for this transition are okay, but the following tips will make the transition work for you...and your clients:

- Keep the effect short; a duration of 15–20 frames works well.

- Change the center of the effect. With the crosshairs, set the center of the effect in a large area of similar color (such as a region of sky or shadows). This will minimize pixilation during the zoom.

- Adjust the Blur setting to Maximum on the effect.

Don't Forget About QuickTime Transitions

Most users avoid the QuickTime transitions folder. We're not sure why—perhaps it's because the transitions are oddly named. Try the following transitions out when you seem to be running low on ideas:

- **Explode:** This warps the outgoing clip into a tunnel-like wipe. We find this particularly useful when going between graphics and an incoming clip. Try offsetting the center of the wipe to match the focal point of the incoming clip.

- **Iris:** The QuickTime Iris transition is worlds better than the Final Cut Pro Iris transition. Choose from 26 different shapes. Particularly nice is the ability to repeat the iris pattern with separate controls horizontally and vertically. Be certain to check this one out.

- **Radial:** With similar options to the Iris transition and 39 patterns to choose from, this effect needs to be on your radar screen.

- **Wipe:** This one transition has more options and possibilities of all the transitions contained in Final Cut Pro's wipe category.

Additive Dissolve: An Effect with No Reason

Perhaps someone far wiser than us can come up for a reason to use the Additive Dissolve. This effect adds the brightest areas up to cause a flare in the middle of the transition. The problem is you always seem to switch into a non-broadcast-safe color space. Just forget this one exists.

While we're at it, what's a Non-Additive Dissolve do? It's really hard to see any difference from Cross Dissolve transition and pretty impossible within one second of playback.

Transitions...Line Up Here

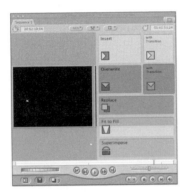

Here's a neat trick: You have a series of clips in your timeline, and you want to add the same transition effect between all of them. Well, if you highlight all the edit points between clips and drop your transition on them, you'll soon discover that Final Cut Pro only puts the transition on the first clip. Not good. Most people we've talked to say this feature is impossible in Final Cut Pro. We disagree.

Create the transitions you want for all these clips, and make it a favorite (in case you want to use it in another show). Then contextual-click on its icon in the bin, and make it your default transition.

Now place the playhead at the beginning of your group of clips. Highlight the group of clips in the timeline that you want, and drag the group up into the canvas. Drop the group on the "overwrite with transition" box. Bam...the clips fall back into the timeline with your default transition between each clip.

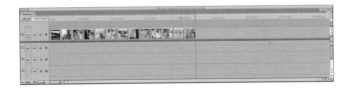 

When to Ripple

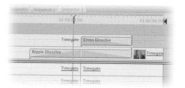

As cool as the Ripple transition is, it has started to look dated (unless your client is an aquarium store). One good use is as a special effect to bring actors into a scene. Simply shoot a locked-down wide shot of your scene. Now have the actors leap into the shot (they can do this from behind the camera, from deep background coming toward you, or from even across frame.) Now use the ripple wipe to transition from the empty locked to the actors in the shot or vice versa. Remember you can use the crosshairs to center the ripple directly over the actors. This is a great way for a "dramatic" entrance.

Turn Off the Telly

Want your video to end like you've pulled the plug? It's not too difficult to simulate a television being switched off.

❶ At the end of your clip, create a segment by adding an edit point.

❷ Load the segment into the viewer by double-clicking.

❸ On the Motion tab, set initial keyframes at the start of the clip for the following categories: Scale, Aspect Ratio, and Opacity.

❹ At the desired end f the transition, add three more keyframes for the aforementioned categories.

❺ Set the Scale keyframe to 20.

❻ Set the Aspect Ratio keyframe to –10000.

❼ Set the Opacity keyframe to 0.

❽ Drag the first Opacity keyframe closer to the second to delay the fade until the effect is approximately halfway completed.

❾ Check the "Motion Blur" box.

To further enhance the effect, consider adding multiple keyframes for opacity and aspect ratio. Better yet, adding the sound of the television clicking off really helps the effect. In Soundtrack you'll find Click Off FX.aiff or Lighter Click FX.aiff, which should work nicely.

ON THE SPOT

Fixing It in Post
Using Color Correction...You Need It!

Lots of folks open up the color corrector, play for a few minutes, get confused by the scopes, and run. Well, after this chapter, the color corrector will be your best friend.

Use color correction as an opportunity to improve your show. It's the polish that really makes a show stand out. Every shot can be tweaked and improved; too little contrast, the wrong color balance, too much saturation, the whites too hot...the list of problems can go on forever. Here's the best part: With the three-way color corrector and its friends, you can often fix these problems in less than a minute!

Read on, and in no time you'll master the three-way color corrector—and start making it do some pretty slick tricks. Pretty soon you'll even know about using composite modes such as Add, Multiply, and Soft Light. This may all seem pretty scary to an editor ("But I'm not a colorist!"), but hang on, we'll get you there.

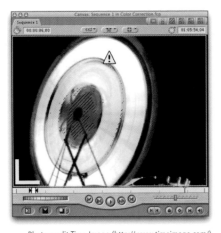

Photo credit Time Image (http://www.timeimage.com/)

Why Is There an Exclamation Point on My Monitor? (Or, Do Zebra Bars Really Grow in My NLE System?)

For those of you in a hurry—and we suspect most of you are—here's a "quick" way to spot problems. Use the Range Check command (View>Range Check). An exclamation point means you have a problem, as do red stripes. Green stripes just mean areas close to the legal limit.

Excess Luma (Ctrl + Z)

If your image is too bright, you'll have problems in a broadcasting environment. Be sure your whites don't exceed their limits. Simply apply a Color Corrector 3-Way filter and pull the Whites slider to the left until the exclamation point goes away. Although the Broadcast Safe filter may fix the luminance problem, most video can afford a few tweaks to the color balance and saturation. That's where the filter really shines.

Excess Chroma

If your image is too saturated, you'll often have colors that bleed (or spread) across the screen. Reds and yellows often have this problem. You can use a Color Corrector 3-Way or the Broadcast Safe filter to fix this problem. Simply desaturate or clamp the illegal colors.

Both

This is how we usually work. We want Final Cut Pro to warn us if there's a problem by popping up the exclamation point. A little work with color correction usually solves the issue. If we have a hard time spotting the trouble area (luminance versus saturation), we'll just switch to one of the specialized views.

Color Corrector 3-Way: Yeah, It's that Easy

The Color Corrector 3-Way filter can solve many problems (and it's fast!). Most people get overwhelmed by the interface, but the key is to use one slider at a time. We usually work in this order to fix a "typical" shot that's not broadcast safe. Make sure your range check is on for both luminance and saturation, and view things on a broadcast monitor if possible.

Photo credit Time Image (http://www.timeimage.com/)

❶ If needed, rebalance the image by sampling with the eyedropper. You may want to turn Range Check off temporarily so you can get a better selection.

❷ Adjust the Whites slider. Slide it slowly to the right until your red zebra stripes disappear.

❸ Slide to the Mids slider to adjust the exposure.

❹ Roll the Blacks slider to the right to restore contrast.

❺ Readjust the Whites slider and then the Mids slider if needed.

❻ Roll a little saturation in (or out) to taste.

Calibrate

If your broadcast monitor isn't calibrated, your color correction is worthless. We freely admit that monitor calibration isn't a forte, and if we wait too long to do it, we usually have to pull out a cheat sheet to remember all the steps. So we'll share this wonderful bit of knowledge with you.

You already own a step-by-step tutorial. It's buried in the *Final Cut Pro User Manual*, Volume III, Appendix D, page 355. Follow the steps–it works!

Photo credit Time Image (http://www.timeimage.com/)

A Simple Clean Up for Digital Video Footage Captured In Low Light

Most people will shoot their video cameras in any type of light, but unfortunately that doesn't always provide the best type of image. Single-chip video cameras were just not made to handle low-light recording, but that doesn't mean you can't use the imagery. So try a trick that digital still photographers use: Run a one- or two-pixel Gaussian Blur filter on just the Blue Video channel. Don't do too much more, or the footage will start to "bloom" or soften in color.

By Gary Adcock, Studio 37, Founder and President of the Chicago FCP User Group

Photo credit Time Image (http://www.timeimage.com/)

Playhead Sync

You've applied color correction to a clip in your timeline and want to access the controls. You double-click the clip, make some adjustments, and go to the next clip. Somewhere along the way you forget to load the clip on which you want to work. Only after several clicks do you discover that you've messed up a shot by color correcting the wrong item.The viewer can now keep up with what you're doing in the timeline automatically. In the viewer, there's a new drop-down menu for playhead sync. Setting the viewer to Open will automatically open the shot at which you're looking. This is very useful for color correction or other effects work.

Quick Adjustments: Gear Up

Most of the time, holding down the Command key slows down your sliders. In the Color Corrector 3-Way filter, it sometimes has the opposite effect. If you're trying to remove colorcast or quickly roll the hue, hold down the Command key to make quick adjustments in the color wheel areas. In other areas of this filter, it serves as a Gear Down command and will slow the dragging of the handles.

Using Eyedroppers: You'll Poke Your Eye Out

Inside the Color Corrector 3-Way, you'll see three eyedroppers in the upper area. These are useful for fixing color balance. Think of this as white balancing in post; we've even fixed video shot on the wrong filter.

Photo credit Time Image (http://www.timeimage.com/)

❶ Use the Whites eyedropper to click on something that should be white. Don't go for the whites of someone's eyes; go with a large area such as a wall.

❷ Use the Blacks eyedropper to click something that should be black.

❸ The Mids eyedropper really only works when using a chip chart or something with 50-percent gray.

❹ If the color balancing is overcompensated, you may need to drag back toward center in the color wheel.

Taking Something Away

Here's a way you can make finely shot footage look aged. In the early days of film, many of the film stocks weren't very saturated with color, and more often the footage had the look of a hand-colored black and white film. Final Cut Pro lets you to get this look in another one of the real-time color correction filters.

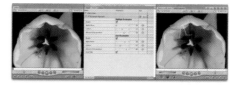

Photo credit Time Image (http://www.timeimage.com/)

Select Filters > Color Correction> Desaturate (Highlights or Lows)—Highlights and Lows are actually the same filter, so don't be confused.

This filter is used to desaturate (or remove) the color in an image higher or lower than the 50-percent luminance threshold. This can create some useful visual transitions if you're coming out from black and white footage or a still image into moving video. Ramping the effects of this filter as part of the transition will give your finished piece a more filmic look.

By Gary Adcock, Studio 37, Founder and President of the Chicago FCP User Group

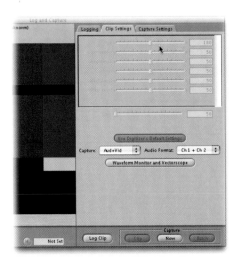

No Adjusting on Diging

Those experienced editors switching to digital systems from older analog systems may go bit nuts during capture. See, they've always been trained to adjust the signal during the capture stage. An experienced editor will twiddle setup knobs on their deck while loading footage into their systems. This has the distinct benefit of minimizing the amount of color correction necessary.

The problem with digital video systems? You can't do this. The video is really just data being sent across a cable. Just as you can't spell check an email as you download it, the same holds true for capturing. For digital video systems, capture first, and then adjust the signal with filters.

Pandora's Box

When the Color Corrector 3-way filter was introduced, there was a lot of confusion. Everyone seemed to be drawn to the controls at the bottom of the screen. They wanted to tweak and fiddle, and pretty soon people started complaining they couldn't get consistent results.

Those controls are for limiting the effect. This is called secondary color correction and is for isolating your touchup to specific areas. Unless that's what you want, don't touch! Fortunately, these are now in a hidden area of the interface of Final Cut Pro 4.

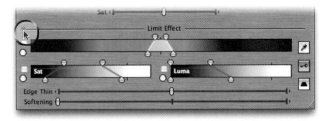

Broadcast Safe (and Lazy...)

Quick, the show you're working on needs to be made broadcast legal. You can afford the render time but not the time necessary to figure out what's legal and what's not. Or maybe you don't know how to read scopes? Whatever.

❶ Create a new sequence with settings that match the sequence that needs fixing. Name it **Safety sequence** to help you know the difference between the two.

❷ Double-click the Safety sequence (so it's open) in the browser.

❸ Select your finished sequence in the Browser. You're going to nest the master sequence (your main sequence you've been working days/weeks/months on) into the new sequence. Drag the master sequence into the safety sequence. This is called nesting and will permit you to put a single effect on the entire show.

❹ In this case, the effect will be the Broadcast Safe effect (Effects>Video Filters> Color Correction> Broadcast Safe). Add this single effect, and it'll make the entire show legal.

❺ Render. Yes, it's a red render bar when played back under Safe RT (in most circumstances). But its presets are pretty conservative and keep most work passing legal requirements.

By Jeff I. Greenberg, Principal Instructor, Future Media Concepts

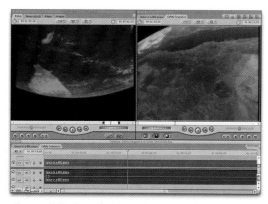

Photo credit Time Image (http://www.timeimage.com/)

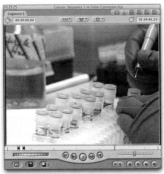

Photo credit Time Image (http://www.timeimage.com/)

Backwards Thinking

When color correcting, you'll often need to see the difference between where you started and where you are. Fortunately, Final Cut Pro 4 adds a new tool for this. Follow these steps:

❶ Switch to color correction arrangement. (Layout-> Arrange -> Color Correction).

❷ Underneath the scopes is the Frame Viewer tab; switch to it.

❸ The Frame Viewer comes up default with a vertical split. On the left is the current frame (green control handles), and on the right is the current frame without any filters.

❹ Switch one of the sides to see the previous frame. Now you can compare your color correction to the previous shot.

By Jeff I. Greenberg, Principal Instructor, Future Media Concepts

Composite Modes: Add It Up

Dark video? That never happens to us, of course, but we hear this is a good fix. If you have a shot that's really dark, you can use screen modes to lift the details out.

❶ Place a cloned copy of the dark shot above itself (Option + drag and then hold down the Shift key).

❷ Contextual-click and change the composite mode. Add works well to combine the lightest elements.

❸ If it's too light, reduce the opacity of the top clip. If it's too dark, clone an additional copy on a third track.

This works great on surveillance/security video, as well.

Your Color Is Garbage (Matte, That Is)

By using two (or possibly three) effects, you can create striking areas of focus. Darkening, brightening, and/or color correcting selective parts of a frame will do this. Essentially, we're using an Eight-Point Garbage Matte effect to create a portion of a clip on top of itself. By using soft edging, it'll blend from the effected area to the unaffected area.

① Clone a copy of the clip above itself in the timeline. Select the clip with the arrow tool, and then drag straight up while holding the Option and the Shift keys.

② On the top clip, add two effects, an Eight Point Garbage Matte (Effects> Video Filters> Matte> Eight-Point Garbage Matte), and a Color Corrector 3-way filter.

③ Load the upper clip in the Viewer, and access the filter controls.

④ Click each of the plus signs after each point (point 1, point 2, and so on), and work your way around the area in the image. Once you click a plus sign, go over to the Canvas, and click and drag until the dot is where you want it to be. You don't have to drag the dot from its initial position–you can just click and hold, and the dot will jump to where you're clicking. It takes a moment as you drag for the screen to update.

⑤ Go down the Filter parameters, and feather and smooth the effect. If you solo the track (V2 in our case), you'll see that only part of the clip is now visible, and it has soft edges.

⑥ Deciding that we're happy with the area, we wanted to darken everything else. We selected the "Invert" checkbox on the Eight-Point Garbage Matte filter, which left us with just the background.

⑦ Before you leave the Eight-Point Garbage Matte effect, make sure to go to the Preview pull-down menu, and select Final.

⑧ Go to the Color Corrector 3-way filter, reduce the saturation, and reduce the Black slider and the Mid slider, making a darker background surrounding a "hole" that saw through to V1.

By Jeff I. Greenberg, Principal Instructor, Future Media Concepts

Photo credit Time Image (http://www.timeimage.com/)

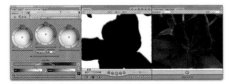

Photo credit Time Image (http://www.timeimage.com/)

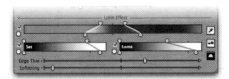

Keyframing

Sometimes problems in a shot just pop in and out (like relatives). Or maybe the color issue changes over time. Don't worry; you can keyframe the color corrector effects to make gradual fixes. In the upper-left corner of the visual interface of the effect is an Insert/Delete keyframe button. By clicking this you'll add a keyframe for all properties. This can be useful if you want to adjust the midtones and saturation to simulate lighting effects over time. In fact, you can even pull off a "time lapse" effect with lighting sources.

A Spot of Color

You can use this specialty effect to add dramatic emphasis to a shot by leaving only one color and stripping the rest. To pull this effect off, you'll need to use the Color Corrector 3-way filter. This effect works best on clip with a dominant color region.

❶ Apply the Color Corrector 3-way filter, and access the filter's visual controls.

❷ Using the Select Color eyedropper in the Limit Effect controls, select the desired color you'd like to keep.

❸ Click the key icon to view the matte. Use the Select Color eyedropper while holding down the Shift key to add to the matte.

❹ Finesse the matte by adjusting the Width and Softness sliders for the Chroma, Saturation, and Luma values in the Limit Effect controls. When the desired color is clearly selected, there will be no holes in your matte.

❺ Click the key icon twice to toggle back to View Final.

❻ Slide the Saturation slider to the left to desaturate the clip.

❼ At the bottom are controls to tweak the effect. Check the "Invert" box at the bottom of the parameters list. Adjust the Thin/Spread and Softening sliders to enhance the effect.

A Frame with a View

There's even more to love about the Frame Viewer:

- The border between the green/handles allows you to change the area where you're splitting the frame.

- The three buttons on the bottom are great:

  - V-Split allows you to vertically split the frame.

  - Swap allows you to swap sides.

  - H-Split allows you to horizontally split the frame.

- The pull-down menus permit you to look a shot ahead or behind to compare the clip you're correcting. This is great for continuity with skin tones.

By Jeff I. Greenberg, Principal Instructor, Future Media Concepts

Photo credit Time Image (http://www.timeimage.com/)

One Hot Spot

Have a problem in just part of your image? There are two approaches worth taking:

- **Broadcast Safe filter:** This filter will clamp the illegal levels and knock them into place. It can sometimes lead to banding, but it's fast and easy to apply.

- **Color Corrector 3-way filter:** A better method is to select the hot spot with the Limit Effect command. Base your selection solely on the luminance (ignoring saturation and hue). Be sure to feather your selection significantly. Now your adjustments to the Mids and Whites sliders will be much gentler.

Photo credit Time Image (http://www.timeimage.com/)

Photo credit Time Image (http://www.timeimage.com/)

Make Your Gray Skies Blue

It's not unusual for your skies to be washed out. This is often a problem because video only supports a low contrast ratio between darks and highlights. By isolating the color correction, you can achieve a fix just to the problem area.

1 Apply the Color Corrector 3-way filter, and access the filter's visual controls.

2 Using the Select Color eyedropper in the Limit Effect controls, select the desired color you'd like to keep.

3 Click the key icon to view the matte. Use the Select Color eyedropper while holding down the Shift key to add to the matte. You can click in the Viewer or Canvas window.

4 Finesse the matte by adjusting the Width and Softness sliders for the Chroma, Saturation, and Luma values in the Limit Effect controls. When the desired color is clearly selected, there will be no holes in your matte. Also adjust the Softening slider to improve the matte.

5 Click the key icon twice to toggle back to View Final.

6 Adjust the color balance wheels and saturation of the shot.

You may need to add a second color corrector to finesse the scene or isolate another problem area.

Photo credit Time Image (http://www.timeimage.com/)

The Ultimate Full-Color Spread

We're about to make your entire screen a mess (it'd be much better at this point to have that Cinema Display or a second screen.) Now that you understand the possibility of the frame viewer, you can have more than one frame viewer. To build an entire layout dedicated to color correction, follow these steps:

❶ Move your viewer down to the lower-left corner (more on that later).

❷ Add scopes and move them to the upper-left corner.

❸ Tearing off the frame viewer, move it to the top row of windows (upper-right corner).

❹ In our screen capture we've already added a color correction effect to the shot. We've changed the Frame Viewer to show Next Edit and Previous Edit. This way we can maintain a "look" from shot to shot.

❺ Rearrange your Viewer on top of the Browser, making sure to just leave a little space to mouse over the Browser if necessary.

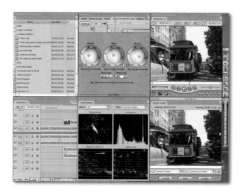

❻ Position the timeline to sit in the bottom right.

❼ Use the up and down keys to go from shot to shot.

❽ The color corrector controls are directly under your scopes… easy for to glance up at.

❾ Is this cramped? Absolutely. Go get a second monitor (or a nice 20-inch, 22-inch, or 23-inch Cinema Display). Most editors swear to having a two-monitor system (and others swear at only having a one-monitor system).

Note: An alternate approach to setting up your windows is also suggested by author Tom Wolsky and is shown in the lower figure. Be sure to experiment and find a layout that works well for you.

By Jeff I. Greenberg, Principal Instructor, Future Media Concepts

Adding Something Back

Too many people forget that the color correction can be used to add more "umphf" to the look of your video. Scenics especially often need some help to make them jump out. Remember, however, this isn't to be used for broadcast because this may cause your video to be out of range.

Select your clip, and then add either the standard or 3-Way Color Corrector filter to it. Open the visual filter version you've selected, and then slide just the saturation sliders over until you get the effect you desire.

By Gary Adcock, Studio 37, Founder and President of the Chicago FCP User Group

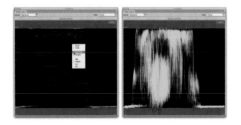

Help! My Scopes are Hard to See...

By default, the scopes in Final Cut Pro use light lines to signify their results. That's fine and all, but that doesn't mean you have to like it. Simply contextual-click a scope, and you can access several different display options that may help you see your results more clearly.

Help! My Scopes are Too Small...

Often times you may want to see multiple scopes as once. You had this option before because Final Cut Pro allowed you to view groupings of scopes. Now, however, you can have more than one scope window. In fact, you can have up to six (which is more windows than unique scopes...go figure). Simply choose Tools >Video Scopes (Option + 9) repeated times to add scopes.

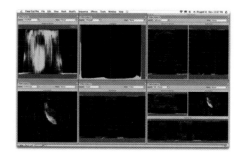

It's a Wash

Need to put some life into washed-out video? Composite modes can be used to increase saturation and contrast. Simply place a cloned copy of a clip on the track above itself, and change its composite mode. Be sure to experiment with the several different modes to get alternative looks.

Photo credit Time Image (http://www.timeimage.com/)

The Faded '60s Color Photo Look

There are many times when an editor is looking to degrade or desaturate the color in video footage or still photos they're using in their project. If they want all the footage to look the same, there's sometimes a problem with color continuity. You may find that still images edited in Adobe Photoshop don't match the video footage edited in Final Cut Pro.

So, you can do both parts in Final Cut Pro to maintain continuity. Save it as a favorite, and then you can apply it to both clips and stills once you have the setting you like.

To make your videos look as if they're faded color photos from the '50s and '60s, select Filters > Color Correction> RGB Balance.

Then try these settings:

	Reds	Greens	Blues
Highlights	341	347	324
Midtones	132	132	127
Blacks	17	−24	6

By Gary Adcock, Studio 37, Founder and President of the Chicago FCP User Group

Color Grading

One of the questions we get all the time about color correction is, "Yeah, but how do I know if there's a problem?" Most people using the range checks quickly learn that their signal needs to fall within a certain range. But that's not where you stop.

Sometimes you need to adjust the colors of a scene for emphasis or narrative purposes. We often modify (or grade) the colors in a scene to add shot-to-shot consistency, as well as to emphasize a mood or feeling. If using color as a major character in your production sounds scary, we suggest you pick up *The Visual Story* by Bruce Block.

Photo credit Time Image (http://www.timeimage.com/)

Joy in Repetition

Although "Joy in Repetition" is a great song (look it up!), the same can't be said for color correction in Final Cut Pro. Let's see, you've color corrected one interview (and it looks great!). At some point, that person is going to pop back into your show.

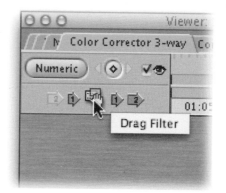

Let's see:

- Same person
- Same location
- Same camera
- Same lighting

We bet you can use the same color corrector. Simply drag the effect icon off to a bin. Name the effect so you can easily find it. Now you can drag the effect preset onto your new clip. Unless something dramatically changed, the effect should work. If you do need to tweak, you're at least five steps closer to "done."

ON THE SPOT

Type-Oh!
Creating Titles That "Work"

"Just slap on a title and get it out the door." These aren't the words that make for a good show. Titles can make or break a show. They're just another one of those "attention to detail" pieces that set you above the pack. We've come to rely on lower-thirds, informational graphics, and title slates to help communicate our messages.

If your text flickers, buzzes, or looks like ants marching across the screen, you need this chapter. If "just put some white letters on the screen, and use that cool Courier font," sounds good to you, then you really need this chapter. A lot of considerations go into choosing the right font, making it readable, and making it fit into your show. And what if you want more? Don't worry; in this chapter, we tackle some of the top issues with Adobe Photoshop and Apple LiveType. We'll get you up and running and on your way to better titles that will make your clients happy.

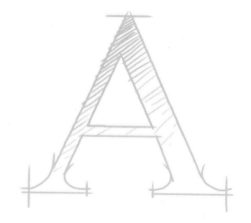

Lose That Umlaut (Symbolically Speaking, Of Course)

Need special characters but can't remember where they live on the keyboard? OS X has a great feature for this, the Character Palette.

❶ Go to System Preferences>International>Input Menu, and enable the Character Palette.

❷ Notice the new icon in your menu bar. When needed, simply choose Show or Hide Character Palette.

❸ Unicode Blocks and the Glyph Catalog are the easiest to browse. The palette automatically floats above your active application.

❹ Be sure to check that you're using the same font in the text generator or other application.

❺ Double-click or drag to use the special character.

You're Glowing...

Making a graphic or text generator "glow" is a nice way to soften its look. This can help reduce the computer-generated "hardness" of the graphic.

❶ Edit the title generator or graphics into your timeline.

❷ Under the Motion tab, apply the Drop Shadow and access its controls.

❸ Set the Offset to 0 to center the glow.

❹ Change the color to match your element, or pick a different color as your light source.

❺ Adjust the Softness and Opacity to taste until the desired effect is achieved.

Templates Are Your Friends

By using a template, you can quickly build repetitive titles with a consistent style. The goal here is to get it right the first time.

Pick a title that's representative of those you'll need. It's a good idea to select the longest title so your template can accommodate all your needs.

Create a new title using a text generator.

When satisfied, drag the title from the viewer to your bin. Be sure to name the clip.

Re-edit the template into the timeline, and then modify each one.

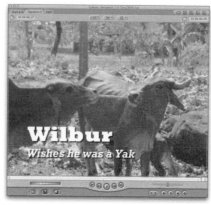

Photo credit James Ball

Better Drop Shadows

When placing type against a moving background, a contrasting edge is a necessity. This is often accomplished by using a drop shadow. But sometimes a drop shadow isn't enough.

❶   Use Outline Text from the Generators well.

❷   Set the line width to a narrower setting (somewhere between 10–25).

❸   Crank the line softness up (40 or higher).

❹   Combine with a Drop Shadow from the Motion tab.

❺   Reduce the Offset value so the shadow is tighter. Increase the Opacity and Softness to taste.

Mostly There (Softening CG Elements)

CG Elements tend to look... computer generated. One way to improve your look when mixing lower-thirds and your video is to reduce the graphic's opacity. Try setting your graphics between 85-percent to 95-percent opacity. This will slightly soften your look and improve readability.

Black Is Black, and White Is White?

You need some titles in your show, so you might as well save some time and build them with the text generators, right? This seems like a good idea, but be careful. It's likely you'll use white and black in your graphic. Using the standard Hue-Saturation-Brightness (HSB) scale, you'll need to use a value of H=0, S=0, and B=90 in order to achieve a video-safe white. For black, you should really use a value of H=0, S=0, and B=6.

Paint with Your Scene

Trying to decide which color to use for your type? Consider using the eyedropper tool to sample color. In the Text Color parameter, you can grab an eyedropper and then pick a color from within your scene. Consider using one of the lighter elements of your scene for white. The color will likely have a small colorcast to it, and that's a good thing. This persistence of color will help tie the graphic and background together.

Black and White Vision

Need to test your graphics for proper contrast? Most designers forget to strip their color away when testing for readability. This is important because several color combinations don't differ significantly when comparing luminance.

❶ Position your playhead over the questionable graphic.

❷ Press Shift + N to create a freeze frame in the viewer.

❸ Select the Viewer.

❹ Strip all color away using Effects> Video Filters> Image Control> Desaturate.

❺ Analyze the graphic for proper readability.

Carve It...(A Better Bevel)

Looking to create a beveled edge? The built-in bevel filter doesn't work on text. Instead, you'll need to use the channels to create the edge.

❶ Choose Effect>Video Filters> Channel> Channel Offset.

❷ Switch the Channel to only move the Alpha Channel.

❸ Offset the channel to taste, usually a value of three to ten pixels for the X and Y axis will work, but you may need to vary this based on the size of your graphic.

❹ Experiment with the Edges settings to refine your look.

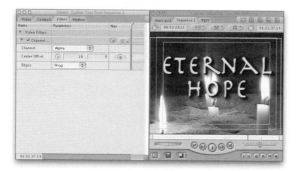

An Approved Color Palette

Need to use certain colors in your show? Make a color strip. In Photoshop, you can create an RGB document that contains blocks of color. By using the Custom Color Picker, you can fill those blocks with Pantone colors. You can also convert from CMYK colors (because most style guides never bother with RGB values). Save this as a single graphic and import into Final Cut Pro. You can now use your eyedropper tool to select colors for use in graphics and generators.

You Must be in the Back Row...

Remember when your mom used to yell at you for sitting too close to the TV? Now look at you, just inches from your edit system's screen all day long. When designing video graphics, you'll likely use type that's entirely too small. Remember, use a larger font and get some distance between you and your monitor. Send the signal out to your deck, then get up, and sit on the client's couch or stand in the back of the room for a while. Review your graphics from a more reasonable vantage point.

A Good Argument for Larger Type

Your computer monitor likely displays 1,000 lines of resolution. A VHS tape can reproduce about 200 lines of resolution. With such a significant loss of quality, be sure to start out with larger type.

LiveType Giving You G5 Envy

Setting your Canvas to Draft quality will improve the speed at which LiveType creates a RAMbased render. This will degrade the quality of the look only for the preview, but it allows LiveType to preview faster because it has to calculate fewer pixels. To access the setting, choose Edit >Project Properties. If you're performing text alignment or kerning, switch to a higher-quality setting.

By Jeff I. Greenberg, Principal Instructor, Future Media Concepts

How to Reclaim 8GB of Space

All that LiveType data sitting on your main hard drive takes up 7.89 gigabytes. If you didn't install it when you installed Final Cut Pro, or if you'd like to install it on an external hard drive, follow these steps:

❶ Open the LiveType DVD 1 and LiveType DVD 2, and copy all the files from LiveType Data into a folder on your external hard drive. Name that folder LiveType Data.

❷ On your main hard drive, place an alias to that folder inside Library >Application Support>LiveType. Call that alias LiveType Data.

❸ When you relaunch, the data will be installed.

By Jeff I. Greenberg, Principal Instructor, Future Media Concepts

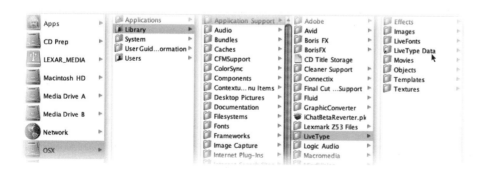

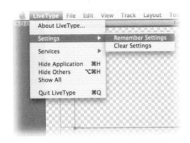

A Permanent Change (Remembering LiveType Settings)

If you've changed your LiveType settings, make this "semipermanent." Choose LiveType> Settings> Remember Settings. Now that you've done this, every future LiveType project starts up the same way.

By Jeff I. Greenberg, Principal Instructor, Future Media Concepts

Stop Wasting Time

When working in LiveType, make sure your duration is the duration of the effect. Drag your In and Out points (or use the keyboard equivalents I and O) to mark the length of time for which you want to preview your effect and create your effect. Only create the time you need!

Make sure, though, that you reset your In and Out points, or your render by default will only cover that preview section.

By Jeff I. Greenberg, Principal Instructor, Future Media Concepts

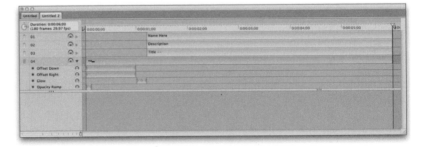

How to Get High "Marks"

You've probably heard that art directors always look for true quote marks (" "). The same holds true for apostrophes or single quotes (' '). But how do you access these when all you have is an engineering-style keyboard? After all, you probably knew that the key next to the Return key was for indicating feet and inches (they look like this, 6' 3").

You access the true quote marks by pressing the following:

Option + [	for	"
Option + Shift + [	for	"
Option +]	for	'
Option + Shift +]	for	'

Important Symbolism

When building screen graphics, there will be several special symbols you'll need. The following table shows a few of the ones clients ask for most. These are on a standard U.S. keyboard, so if you can't find something, fire open KeyCaps from your Utilities folder. And, remember, not all fonts have full character sets (especially the cheap sets).

Symbol	Key Combination	Name
•	Option + 8	Bullet
TM	Option + 2	Trademark
¢	Option + 4	Cents
°	Option + Shift + 8	Degrees
´	Option + E + Letter	Accent
®	Option + R	Registered
©	Option + G	Copyright
√	Option + V	Check Mark
	Option + Shift + K	Apple

"Hello"
He's
6' 3"

91

Side by Side Credit Roll

We've seen people jump through some amazing hoops to perform side-by-side credit rolls. They do one credit roll for the tile justified right, then move left, and do another credit roll with the name justified left, and then move right. Then aligned…and the horror continues.

Actually, it's very easy. Open the Scrolling Text option under Text in the generator's tab or Effect tab. Simply type the person's title, then an asterisk (*) with no spaces, and then the person's name. You'll see that your list has them right and left justified to each other. And that mysterious "gap width" slider now does something. (This only works with center-justified scrolling text.)

Oh, Heaven Let Your Light Shine Down

Did you know you can use Video Generators and Composite Modes to create a sweeping shine effect on titles and graphics? You just need a title or full-screen graphic with an alpha channel.

1 In a new sequence, edit the graphic into V1.

2 From the Video Generators menu, load a Highlight from the Render category. Superimpose the Highlight into V2 above the graphic.

3 Double-click the Highlight in the timeline so its settings load into the Viewer. In its Controls tab, adjust the Highlight Angle and Width settings to determine the look of the shine, and animate the Center parameter to move it across the screen.

4 Control + click the Highlight segment in the timeline, and choose Composite Mode > Travel Matte - Alpha. The Highlight should now only be visible within the shape of the graphic's alpha channel. If you want the shine to seep along the edges of the alpha and glow more, apply a Gaussian Blur filter to the graphic, and increase the Radius setting.

5 Select the two segments in the timeline, and hit Option + C to nest them together. Name the nest something such as Highlight Shape Nest.

6. From the Browser, superimpose the original graphic onto V2 directly above the Highlight Shape Nest.

7. Control + click the graphic, and experiment with different Composite Modes to blend the shine into the graphic. Depending on the colors in your graphic, you may get the best results with the Add, Multiply, Screen, Hard Light, or Soft Light options.

By Christopher Phrommayon, Future Media Concepts

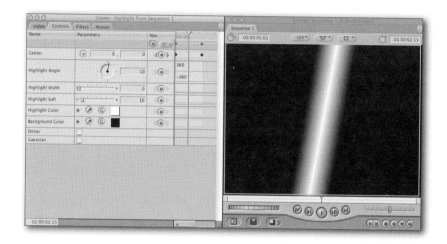

Save Everything

LiveType will not cover you automatically with an Autosave feature. So, be sure to frequently save your work. While on the topic of saving, is your client going to ask for a change? Always save your LiveType project, and you'll be able to go back and change the font, the text you may have misspelled, or the person who has been promoted.

By Jeff I. Greenberg, Principal Instructor, Future Media Concepts

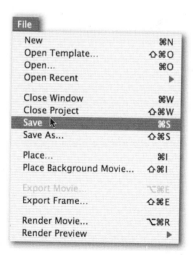

Outline Text

The outline text tool in the Generators tab is one of our favorite text generators to make good-looking titles right inside Final Cut Pro. It automatically puts an outline around your text so that it punches out of your background video no matter how light or dark the video is.

When you begin, the line width default of 50 is way too thick. Move the slider to about 10. Depending on your font and type size, you may need to adjust the tracking so letters don't collide with their neighbors.

Remember you can change the colors of the interior of the letters, the edge, and the background. Background is pretty cool. You can move the sliders at the bottom of the control tab in Background Settings to create a bar behind your title. Soften the edges, adjust the color, and adjust the opacity—you'll get a really nice-looking title.

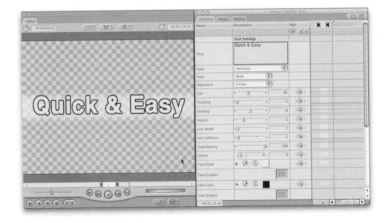

Outline Text Part II - Graphic Wells

Our favorite untapped elements of the outline text tool are the Wells. Wells? Yes, those three little gray squares with the filmstrip and the question marks in them. They're labeled Text, Line, and Back Graphic. If you drop any graphic into these wells, the graphic will be mapped onto the text, the outline area, or the background. You can even drop a video clip into the well, and Final Cut Pro will map the first frame of the movie.

Oh yeah, to remove an image from a well, control + click it!

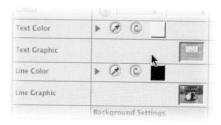

LiveType Shapes

In LiveType, you'll often find secrets if you "dig." Look closely in the Description area of LiveFonts. You'll often find special shapes or looping commands listed. Follow the directions, and you'll get new things.

Speaking of new things, wonder why the engineer liked his old iPod so much?

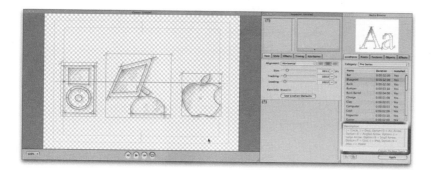

ON THE SPOT

PLACE YOUR HANDS "HERE"

JUST A LITTLE BIT...HOW TO TRIM

JUMP AROUND

INSIDE OUT (MARKS YOU NEED)

GIVING THANKS

BEST PLACE TO START

SELECTIVE ZOOM

I AM THE KEYMASTER

TIME ON YOUR SIDE

BUTTONS ON THE MOVE

MAKING A BETTER BROWSER

SAVING WINDOW LAYOUTS

MISS THE POWER BUTTON?

BUTTON...BUTTON

THE TERMINATOR

GONE BUTTON CRAZY

COME ON OVER TO MY PAD

IS IT SAFE?

STARTUP COMMANDS

THE ENTIRE PICTURE: NO MORE, NO LESS

CHAPTER 7

One-Click Wonders
Using Buttons and Keyboard Shortcuts

Time is money…and we all like money! This chapter shows you how to save time, even a few seconds here and a minute there. Nothing impresses a client more than the sound of keys banging and buttons clicking when they request a change or an effect.

If a client sees you using pull-down windows, they assume you're hunting (and that anyone can edit). Heck, anyone can use a pull-down window! Clients completely forget there's skill and art involved with editing.

With the advent of a mappable keyboard and the ability to create custom buttons, Final Cut Pro has become the uber–editing application we all want. In this chapter, we'll show you some of the best secrets for increasing your productivity, impressing your clients, and making a few extra bucks. Hey, if these tips make you 2-percent faster, you'll save an hour a week. That's more than 50 hours a year, an extra week of vacation. So, where are we going?

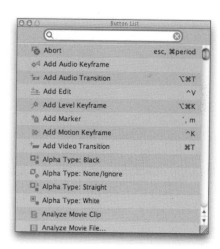

Place Your Hands "Here"

When editing on a desktop system, it's important to think ergonomically. Proper hand position improves your speed and cuts down on work-related pain. When editing, try placing your hands in the following position.

❶ Place the mouse in your preferred hand.

❶ Offset the keyboard so the J-K-L keys fall directly under your opposite hand.

Why? Well, you can access 90 percent of the edit commands from this position.

J	Play Reverse. Tap J to go faster.
K	Pause. Hold K down while using J or L to play in slow- motion.
L	Play Forward. Tap L to go faster.
I	In
O	Out
F9	Insert
F10	Overwrite

Add the Shift, Option, and Command keys for several additional options that speed up editing. In fact, the neighboring keys all hold key commands by default; this is definitely 'prime real estate' in the editing world.

Just a Little Bit...How to Trim

Trim commands are at your fingertips, as well. You can perform single frame trims by tapping the following keys:

, or [	Trim – 1 Frame
. or]	Trim + 1 Frame
Shift + , or [	Trim Minus Many Frames
Shift + . or]	Trim Plus Many Frames

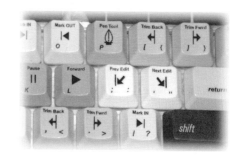

In Final Cut Pro 4, you can set the Multi-Frame Trim Size to be up to 99 frames. We find that using a 10-frame or 15-frame trim size is the most useful for NTSC projects. These work because they translate to 1/3- and 1/2-second trims. So if you're working in PAL 25 frames per second or film 24 frames per second, you may want to adjust accordingly.

Jump Around

Need to give your pinky something to do? When your fingers are on the J-K-L keys, your pinky can hit the semicolon (;) and quote (') keys to jump to the previous and next edits, respectively.

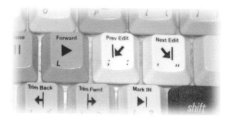

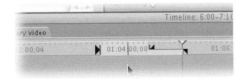

Inside Out (Marks You Need)

A fundamental keyboard shortcut is using I to mark an In point and O to mark an Out point. In fact, three-point editing is the key to quickly (and accurately) assembling your rough cut. Want to really speed your way through the viewer and canvas? Try the following advanced keyboard options.

Modifier Key	I	O	Purpose
Shift	Go to In	Go to Out	Quickly jump to the set mark. Useful for checking points before making an edit.
Option	Clear In	Clear Out	Quickly clear a mark to change an edit. You don't need to clear a mark if you're going to make a new mark.
Control	Set video In point	Set video Out point	Useful for performing a split edit. Only visible if a separate audio In point is set.
Command + Option	Set audio In point	Set audio Out point	Allows you to make a split edit where the audio and picture change at different points.

Giving Thanks

Thanks to the new customizable keyboard, you can create keyboard shortcuts where none existed before. And thanks to the new button creation tool, you can create quick button shortcuts on the timeline of your favorite keyboard shortcuts.

Best Place to Start

Two keyboard shortcuts to learn before moving forward in this chapter are Option + H to open the Customize Keyboard Layout window and Option + J to open the Button List window. Of course, your first exercise could be to make buttons for both of these commands.

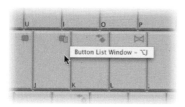 

Selective Zoom

Suppose you want to zoom in to just a few clips. Simply highlight them (Shift + select or lasso them), and then press Option + Shift + Z. Boom...you zoom into just those clips in your timeline.

I am the Keymaster

Want to know all the keyboard shortcuts? Call up the Custom Keyboard Layout window. On each tab, you can roll over each key and learn what that key can do. When you've memorized all those (call us if you do), switch to the button list and start on those. By then, version 6 will be out.

Time on Your Side

Apple chose to bury the time remap tool in the toolbar with the slip and slide tool.

We think it's a lot more convenient to have the Time Remap Tool button right on our Timelines, so we just put one there. Go to Tools > Button List to open the button dialog box. Type the word **time**, grab the Time Remap Tool button, and drag it to the Timeline. While you're there, grab the Time Code Overlay button, the Zoom in to Timeline button, and the Zoom out of Timeline buttons. These work beautifully on your Timeline window, as well.

Buttons on the Move

A lot of folks know how to bring a button to a button bar and can readily move them from bar to bar, but they don't realize you can copy a button from one bar to another by Option + dragging it to the new bar.

Browsing Buttons (Making a Better Browser)

Our favorite buttons to put on the Browser bar are Long Frames: Mark and Analyze Movie. Doing this, you can quickly highlight one or a group of clips and see if you've dropped frames or have other problems...all with one click.

Saving Window Layouts 14

When we present Final Cut Pro, we tend to drag windows all over the place. As a matter of fact, we do it when we edit, too. Our desktop becomes a real mess! It's nice to be able to quickly revert to a nice clean layout. Final Cut Pro 4 allows you to save your window layouts simply and quickly by going to Window> Arrange > Save Window Layout. But there's no keyboard shortcut, so assign one. We use Shift + Command + U. We like this combination because it works well with the restore layout combination Shift + Option + U. Of course, to be really efficient, we make a button to save the window layout right on our timeline bar.

Now the fun begins. Create buttons for all your custom window layouts. You can be as messy as you want and with one click—instant maid service—you'll have a nice, clean layout. If only we could create a button like this for our kitchens!

Miss the Power Button?

For those of you longing for your old keyboard, here are a few good shortcuts that work from the Finder:

Sleep, Restart, Shutdown dialog box	Control-Eject
Restart	Command-Control-Eject
Sleep	Command-Option-Eject
Shutdown	Command-Control-Option-Eject

Gary Adcock, Studio 37, Founder and President of the Chicago FCP User Group

Button... Button

Want to create a button for your favorite keyboard shortcut, but you can't remember its name? No worries—you can search the button list by typing the keyboard shortcut into the search field. You can now simply drag the button to the button bar of your choice.

The Terminator

Does contextual-clicking to remove a button seem too slow? Just drag the button off the bar. Poof...up in smoke.

Gone Button Crazy

You can tell by now that we're pretty giddy over the option to create lot and lots of buttons. Well, here's a tip to manage them: You can contextual-click any button, change its color, and even put spacers between them. (Psst...you can even give a color label to the spacers.)

Here's the kicker: You can save and reload button sets. This allows you to create one set for basic editing, one for finessing your edit, one for color correction, one for audio mixing, one for...well, you get the picture.

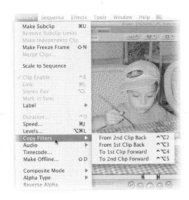

Come On Over to My Pad

All of these button and keyboard shortcuts work well for us, but we realize each editor is unique. Here's a tip about how to customize Final Cut Pro to meet your workflow: Keep a pad of paper next to your computer. Any color will do…we like yellow. Use the application heavily for about a week. Now, every time you go to a pull-down menu, write it down. Then add a check mark each time your return to that menu action. After a good 40 hours of use, you'll have a real good idea of what buttons and shortcuts will work for you.

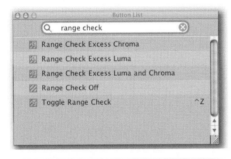

Is it Safe?

The range check tool, which was added in version 3, is great to make sure your shots are broadcast safe. We always thought it'd be nice to be able to quickly toggle "range check" on and off for excess luma and chroma. With the button tool in Final Cut Pro 4, now we can. Search for "range check" in the button list, and drag the set of three buttons to the bar above the Canvas. While you're in the Customize Button window, type **title safe**, and drag that button next to the excess luma and chroma buttons. Now you'll know when it's safe during your editing marathons…Man!

Startup commands

Need to get things off to a good start?

Force Mac OS X startup	Hold down X during startup
Select a hard drive to boot from	Hold down Option during startup
Start up from a CD (with a system folder)	Hold down C during startup
Start up in FireWire Target Disk Mode	Hold down T during startup
Start up from a network server	Hold down N during startup

Gary Adcock, Studio 37, Founder and President of the Chicago FCP User Group

The Entire Picture: No More, No Less

Want to see the entire picture—no more, no less? Press Shift + Z while working in the canvas or viewer, and the video will Fit to Window. Try this in the timeline, and you can see your entire program. This tip works in the Viewer and the Canvas because if the picture isn't sized to the window (or smaller), you won't get proper playback.

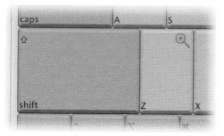

ON THE SPOT

Sounds Good
Enhancing and Troubleshooting Audio

Audio provides more than 70 percent of the experience when watching a video or movie. If the picture is less than perfect but the audio is clear, people will watch. Conversely, if the audio is poor and the picture is great, they'll get weary of fighting to hear and give up.

In this chapter, we'll show you how to clean up poor audio, make sure your levels are balanced, and teach you how to build a soundstage with the panning controls.

The biggest mistake for first-time filmmakers and directors is a flat, uninteresting audio bed. The richer your audio mix, the more professional your finished show will feel. So go ahead, take advantage of some of those 99 audio layers, keyframe the pan and volume sliders, and of course enjoy those real-time audio filters. We're listening!

Telephone Effect

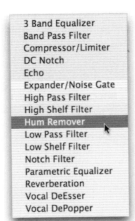

So you need to make it sound as if someone is talking on the telephone? The filter you want is the High Pass filter. It only lets the high-frequency sounds pass through, get it? Some folks like to use the Band Pass filter for this effect. It allows you to modify a single-frequency band. By choosing its center frequency, you can modify the boost or cut level.

The best thing about Final Cut Pro 4 is that you can play your clip and adjust the filter in real-time until it sounds just like a telephone. This trick is also useful if you've aged your video to look like an old film, and you want to pull out some bass so the audio matches the "age" of the pictures.

Hum Remover

This is a great little filter to remove AC noise from a track. Usually this happens because a power line was running parallel (as opposed to perpendicular) to your audio cable when you recorded your scene.

● Leave the frequency set to 60 (as in 60 cycles) if you were shooting in the U.S. or set it to 50 if you were shooting in a country where the power is 50 cycles.

● Q is the attack time, and a gain is sound pressure level (a.k.a. how loud the audio is).

What about all those harmonics? Think of them as reflections or echoes of the original 60-cycle hum. Use only the harmonics you need because you may start removing frequencies you want in your audio.

I Can't Hear You... (Part One)

A clip is low, so you bring the gain up. But you can only do so +12db. What's a frustrated editor to do? Well, you have two choices:

- Mix the track to +12db.

- Duplicate the track by placing a copy of the clip(s) immediately below it. Select the desired clip, and then hold down Option + Shift. Drag directly below the currently selected clip.

This additive method will essentially "double" the sound. If it's now too "hot," then lower the levels on one of the tracks.

I Can't Hear You... (Part Two)

If track space is a concern, you can try nesting. This will allow you to increase the overall mix without consuming timeline real estate:

1. First, mix the track as loud as you can.

2. Second, highlight the clip in need of additional gain.

3. Next, choose Sequence | Nest Items (Option + C).

4. Then highlight the clip, and press Enter to load it into the viewer.

5. Finally, adjust the gain up to an additional +12db.

Hey, They Panned My Show!

Sound provides dimension to your project. By panning audio you can create a sound space that can envelop your viewer. Cars can scream by left to right in your chase scenes. Stereo music from a band can become more centered as the camera pulls back from the stage, and you can have the audio follow your actors as they walk around in the shot.

● You can pan your audio in three places in Final Cut Pro 4:

● In the audio tab of the viewer. (It's the dark purple line.)

● In the timeline. You need to toggle on the "clip overlays" feature in the timeline. (Control + click in the blank area once you see the keyframe area. Again, it's the dark purple line.)

● In the Audio Mixer tab of the tool bench window (the horizontal sliders below the headphone and speaker icons in each column).

Audio Insurance is the best policy

Here's a recording trick we use in the field: If we're recording an interview or speaker from a single mike, we run the same feed into both audio channels. On the second channel, we reduce the recording levels by 3db. This way, if the speaker gets too enthusiastic and spikes their audio past 0db on channel one, we have a –3db insurance policy on channel two.

The Key to better panning

Remember, you can keyframe panning in all three areas. If you toggle on the Record Audio Keyframes button (Shift + Command + K) in the audio mixer or the preferences, you can pan on the fly. Think of them as flying pans...duck!

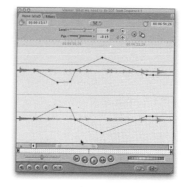

Got to Split Your Tracks

If you recorded your audio in stereo and want to pan you tracks individually, then use the Modify pull-down menu to split the tracks (uncheck Stereo Pair under the Modify menu or press Option + L) and pan them to the center (Modify> Audio> Pan Center (Control + period)). Now you're ready to go.

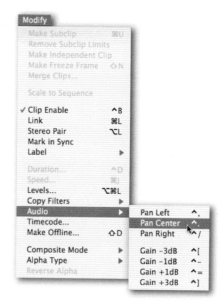

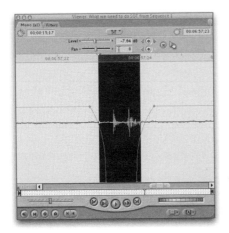

Pop Killer

For one reason or another you may get an audio pop at the edit point or even within a clip. Most video applications allow you to edit video at the frame level. Final Cut Pro goes way beyond this by allowing audio edits as small as 1/100th of a frame.

1 Open the clip in the Viewer by double-clicking, and choose the Audio tab.

2 Place the playhead over the click.

3 Zoom in as far as possible by pressing Command + +. When zoomed in all the way, you'll see a highlighted region that's one frame wide.

4 Hold the Shift key down, and drag the playhead. Park over the exact place where the pop appears.

5 Use the Pen tool to add four keyframes in a row. The center two keyframes should straddle the audio problem. The outer keyframes are placed a few 100ths of a frame from the pop.

6 Drag the inner keyframes down to –60db. The unwanted noise should now be inaudible. The rest of the clip should sound unaltered.

Capture Settings

When you capture audio from DV, you can choose Ch 1 + Ch 2, Ch 1 (L), Ch 2 (R), Stereo and Mono Mix. But don't panic if you picked the wrong setting. Because DV is all 0s and 1s, these settings determine how Final Cut Pro will interpret the audio. So you brought the clip in as stereo and you want discreet channels—just uncheck Stereo Pair under the Modify menu. And, of course, you link your discreet channels back together using the same modifier.

High Pass vs. Low Pass

High pass was what our parents expected of us in college…low pass was what we did to eek by. When it comes to filters, these guys are opposite sides of the same coin.

The High Pass filter is designed to reduce low frequencies, leaving high frequencies alone. It's useful for reducing traffic rumble or airplane noise in a clip.

The Low Pass filter is designed to reduce high frequencies, leaving low frequencies alone. It's great for toning down a sound that's too "bright" and reducing things like tape hiss and machine noise from a clip.

AUBandpass
AUDelay
AUGraphicEQ
AUHighShelfFilter
AUHipass
AULowpass
AULowShelfFilter
AUParametricEQ
AUPeakLimiter

Where To? (Getting the Right Mix)

There's a lot of confusion when looking at the Audio Meter. Unlike the analog world, you DO NOT want to mix to 0db. What this means is that you'll likely need to adjust audio per clip.

- For a digital mix, you want to be near –12db when your output is videotape.

- If you're going to the Internet, you can mix it hotter for playback on computer speakers.

- If you're "seeing red" in your audiometers, your audio is distorted.

- Even though your individual tracks may be at proper levels, when you combine tracks in the timeline, the overall volume "adds up." Keep a careful eye (and ear) on your final mix.

Reverb or Echo?

So what's the difference between the Reverb filter and the Echo filter? Reverb takes place inside a space, such as in a room (with walls and such). Echo takes place in the great outdoors…amphitheaters, grand canyons, and baseball stadiums –adiums- iums- ms-s. Well you get the idea. Be careful because these filters can quickly go from effective to cheesy.

Compressor/Limiter and the AU Peak Limiter

Both the Compressor/Limiter filter and the AU Peak Limiter filter are designed to smooth out inconsistencies in volume levels, consistently across all frequencies. Compression of volume reduces the dynamic range so that it doesn't become too loud. The attack and decay settings specify how fast this effect should adjust the volume levels.

The Compressor/Limiter filter has Threshold and Preserve Volume options. After making settings, use the Preserve Volume option to keep the overall level close to the original. The Threshold setting specifies the level at which the effect will be triggered.

It All Adds Up

You can test this yourself by taking bars and tone and putting them on A1 and A2; you'll find that it reads –12 digitally. If you add a second instance of bars and tone so the tone is also on A3 and A4, you'll find your audio is now –6 digitally, each instance adding –3.

This can be a serious problem; audio levels can combine and be louder summed than they are indivudually. Final Cut Pro's Mark Audio Peaks (Mark > Audio Peaks -> Mark) is meant to point this out to you. It'll find all instances where a clip exceeds 0 and hence is adding distortion into your mix.

However, the feature doesn't work correctly. It marks an audio peak of a clip, but you need it to mark an audio peak of the sum of the clips to prevent peaking of the sequence. Any peak that occurs digitally will cause digitial noise when played back out to tape. Follow these steps:

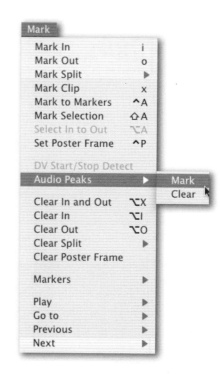

❶ Create a new sequence.

❷ Drag your existing master sequence into this new sequence.

❸ Go to Mark > Audio Peaks > Mark.

❹ Audio peaks are now detected on your timeline. Be sure to visually note where the problem areas are.

❺ Double-click your master sequence now in your audio peaks sequence to open the original and make volume adjustments to repair the peaks.

❻ Return to the audio peaks sequence, go to Mark > Audio Peaks > Clear, and check for marks again.

Jeff I. Greenberg, Principal Instructor, Future Media Concepts

That Music is HOT...Too Hot!

We talked about mixing to –12 db when you edit to DV (–18 or –20 db for digibeta), but people often forget that music they convert and insert off music CDs is mixed to –0db. (Yes, we meant to say the – before the zero. That's because music CDs are mixed and compressed so they sound nice and loud in your car and on your iPod; they peak right below 0db.)

Remember, whenever you use music from a CD, pull its levels down so they hit the appropriate (–12 or –20db) target levels of your show.

Your Professional Music Tool

The audio tool that sees the most use in our studios is iTunes (and not just because we're addicted to the iTunes Music Store). iTunes has several features that are useful to a video pro (and you can't beat the price!). Here are two great uses for this great application:

Create selects CDs: Use iTunes to create listening discs for your clients. This way, you can organize and deliver several tracks from stock music libraries or from Soundtrack. Simply create a playlist of your tracks, and be sure to label each track clearly. Burn the playlist, and deliver it to your client in a format they can listen to in their car or at the gym. Now when they call to say they want you to use track 7, you're both on the same page.

Encode the rough cut: Client in a remote location (or producer "too busy" to come to the edit suite)? You can make an MP3 of the rough cut and email it. Often times, approval on the A-roll is really just a sign-off that the right sound bites are being used and the rough mix is acceptable. Simply create an AIFF file, and use iTunes to convert it to an MP3. The VBR encoding and Joint Stereo features on the Import tab offer superior file size.

Get the Drop on Digital Audio

Final Cut Pro can handling using different imported audio (almost always CDs or MP3s), but by converting its to the same rate as your project– (DV would be 48kHz, 16-bit, Stereo–it's possible not to use up any of Final Cut Pro's real-time audio abilities for the conversion. This will free up RAM for other purposes. Let's make a droplet, so all of this in the future becomes drag and drop.

❶ Launch the compressor, and click the Presets icon.

❷ Add an AIFF preset (alternatively, you could add a folder to group any custom Compressor settings you make).

❸ Double-click to rename the new preset (something such as **Audio 48kHz conversion**).

❹ Click the Encoder tab.

❺ Click the Settings button.

❻ Adjust the settings to no compression, 48kHz, 16-bit, Stereo.

❼ Click OK, and you now have a prebuilt setting. All that's left is to make a droplet.

❽ Click the Save Selection As Droplet (with the new converter selected).

❾ Choose where you want the droplet to be saved and where you want its output to go.

❿ We couldn't get the droplet "drag-and-drop" feature truly working. We had to double-click the droplet, drag the groups of files to the source window, and click Submit to get the custom droplet to work reliably. The reason is that OS X doesn't know that the MP3 or AIFF format might belong to this droplet. If you make a mistake in what you drag into the droplet, just quit it and relaunch it.

Jeff I. Greenberg, Principal Instructor, Future Media Concepts

Audio 48 kHz

CDs Get Converted

Our favorite way to rip and up-convert music from stock music CDs is to use iTunes.

We all know music CDs are recorded at a sampling rate of 44.1kHz. Final Cut Pro and digital video love to work at a sampling rate of 48kHz. Yes, we know Final Cut Pro 4 can up-sample on the fly, but why waste CPU power that could be going to your real-time video playback?

Here's all you need to do:

❶ Open iTunes.

❷ Open Preferences under the Edit menu.

❸ Click the importing icon on the toolbar.

❹ Under Import Using, select AIFF Encoder.

❺ Under Setting, select Custom.

❻ Another dialog box opens. Here, select a sample rate of 48.000 kHz. Click OK and then OK again.

❼ Now click the advanced icon on the menu bar.

❽ Under iTunes Music Folder Location, change it to target your desktop. (This will make it real easy to find and move your newly ripped tracks.)

❾ Pop in your CD. If you're connected to the Internet, iTunes will go to the CDDB and grab the album name and track names. (Yes, it seem as if most of our library music is listed in the CDDB.) This is great because most of the work is done. Create a playlist of all the tracks you want to rip.

❿ Click Import, and you're done!

Once you've set up your preferences, just "rip and roll" every time you need to grab a music cut. Fast, easy, elegant...and of course...cool.

Force Fitting Audio

Your narration for your 30-second spot runs 32 seconds. No matter how you slice and dice it, you can't cut out one frame.

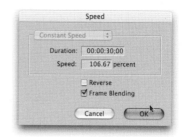

❶   Open the clip, and drop it into the viewer.

❷   Press Command + J to open the Speed window, and reset the duration to 30 seconds.

❸   Now drop the clip back into the browser.

❹   Control + click the new version, and make it a master clip, renaming the clip so you know it's the modified version.

Okay, that works great, but you've changed the pitch of the narrator's voice to be a bit higher. If it still sounds okay, run with it. If not, try using an equalizer to push the lower frequencies louder.

Don't Have a Hissy

Few people really understand the Vocal DeEsser or Vocal DePopper filters. Who are these guys, and why are they in my Audio Filters tab? These two filters are there to help your audio narrations. They literally do what they sound like they do. The Vocal DeEsser removes sibilance from your narrations...those hard "s" sounds that make your narrators sound "hissy." The Vocal DePopper controls and dampens the explosive ("p") sounds that result from bursts of air hitting the microphone when saying sentences such as "Peter Piper picked a peck of pickled peppers."

3 Band Equalizer
Band Pass Filter
Compressor/Limiter
DC Notch
Echo
Expander/Noise Gate
High Pass Filter
High Shelf Filter
Hum Remover
Low Pass Filter
Low Shelf Filter
Notch Filter
Parametric Equalizer
Reverberation
Vocal DeEsser
Vocal DePopper

MTV-Style Slo-Mo

This is really pretty cool way to create a music video or create a disturbing film effect. Prior to filming/videotaping, take your music track and speed it up (2¥–3¥). Lay it back to tape or CD. Now when your talent lip-syncs to the audio during the shoot, they'll be lip-syncing to some really fast music.

Take the captured footage, and slow it down to 1/2 or 1/3 speed–the reverse of the amount you sped up the original tracks.

What the viewer sees and hears is the normal audio, in perfect sync with the video– except the video is now going in slow motion. If you listen closely, you can hear your viewers say, "Whoa, how did they do that?"

A Little Louder Please...

Need to tweak the mix a little? You can quickly change the volume of a highlighted track from the keyboard. Use the following keyboard combinations to perfect the mix:

Gain **–3db**	Control [
Gain **–1db**	Control –
Gain **+1db**	Control +
Gain **+3db**	Control]

A Better Musical Bed

Because of timing or budget constraints, you can't involve an audio editor to "sweeten" your audio mix. Audio mixing is where almost all NLE editors are weakest. Sitting in front of your system, you use a general-level mix adjustment or keyframing to adjust the levels to "mix" the audio. The simplest example is narration or dialogue against music. You bring the music down to accommodate the voice.

A better idea is to lower the range of the music that interferes with the vocal spectrum.

The human voice (the important parts of it anyway) exists from around 500hz through about 2000hz (or 2kHz.) You can lower the music to create a "pillow" for the vocal ranges to exist.

Why the music? If it's a large track, it's easy to make one adjustment rather than hundreds. It's still permissible to also use levels or keyframing on the music track.

Using a parametric equalizer, it's possible to dampen the music inside of the audio spectrum where the vocal ranges exist. A parametric equalizer has a Q value—a value that permits the effect to adjust a wider or narrower band of frequencies. With it set low, a wider set of frequencies are affected; with a Q set high, a very narrow band, or "notch," is affected.

First, select the track(s) on the timeline you want to apply the Parametric EQ filter to, choose it from the Effects menu, double-click the track, and go to the viewer to adjust the controls.

Adjust the frequency to be halfway between 500 and 2,000, setting it to 1250. You can then drop the gain of that selection of the sound spectrum down –18 decibels. With a little experimenting, we found that a Q setting of 4 was acceptable for us. (No, Final Cut Pro doesn't have that visual indicator, but a little bit of listening and patience was enough.)

And there you go. You'll get music that's strong, along with vocal tracks that are intelligible. Would you prefer an experienced audio editor looking at your work? Absolutely! But when you're a one-man band or the budget isn't there, then a little bit of sweetening goes a long way.

Jeff I. Greenberg, Principal Instructor, Future Media Concepts

WOW 99 Sliders Audio Mixer - Gotchas and Shortcuts

Final Cut Pro 4 has a great new feature that lets you mix up to 99 track of audio using sliders. Here are some tricks to make it work faster and better:

● Remember to activate the Record Audio Keyframes button (Shift + Command + K).

● For a smoother mix, choose to record reduced keyframes only.

● If you haven't already done this, create a set of buttons (Audio Keyframe Recording Group in the audio mixer to let you toggle between All, Reduced, and Peaks Only).

● Create a button for "audio mixing" that automatically resets your windows for audio mixing. We put ours on the canvas of the timeline.

● Create a button for "audio mixing" that just opens up the tool bench window with the Audio Mixing tab open.

Record Audio Keyframes

This one bears repeating: If your Record Audio Keyframes feature isn't on, all you do is change levels between keyframes, not create new keyframe points. Also, remember you can choose to adjust multiple tracks, but you can only manipulate one slider (or pair) with the mouse at a time.

Copy Paste Attributes

You can currently only record keyframes for one stereo pair or mono track at a time. If you want to map these keyframes onto another set of tracks, simply copy and then select Paste Attributes (under the Edit menu or press Option + V.) The trick is to uncheck the "Scale Attribute Times" option. This way your keyframes will match up whether the clip lengths are the same (assuming you had them both start at the same time).

Making Waves

Many editors find audio waveforms helpful when editing. You've likely noticed the waveforms in your Viewer menu. It's possible to view this same information directly in the timeline:

❶ Highlight the Timeline or Canvas, and press Command + 0 to access the timeline settings.

❷ Select the Timeline Options tab.

❸ Check the "Show Audio Waveforms" box.

❹ Make the desired tracks larger to see the audio waveform data in the timeline.

Final Cut Pro 4 makes this even easier by adding this command to the Timeline Options submenu. Simply click the submenu at the bottom of the timeline, and choose Show Audio Waveforms.

Better yet, press Command + Option + W to toggle waveforms on or off. Be sure to turn these off when not in use because they slow down the timeline's ability to redraw.

Audio Playback Quality Preference

This can be a confusing preference setting (under User Preferences.) Your first reaction may be to set this to High (versus the default of Low.) However, the Low setting is what you want. This preference setting is only used while you're editing. So it'll give you a close but not perfect approximation of your mix. If you switch it to High, ...guess what, you'll probably get those annoying little beeps, and your audio may need to be rendered to be heard (in that case, choose to mixdown your audio in advance).

When you're ready to print to tape or edit to tape, Final Cut Pro automatically renders your audio at full resolution. One word of warning, though: If you perform crash records directly from the timeline, your audio will play back at low resolution.

Seeing Red...Boxes, That Is

If you have little red boxes with small numbers in them on your timeline, Final Cut Pro is telling you that your audio and video are out of sync. It's even telling you by how much. What we love about this feature is that to fix the problem all you need to do is Control + click the box (either in the video or audio track), and Final Cut Pro will do the math to slip or move your audio and video into sync. If you Control + click the red box in the video, Final Cut Pro will move or slip the video. And if you Control + click the audio, well, you guessed it—the audio moves or slip. If an option is grayed out, that means there would be a clip collision if the media were moved.

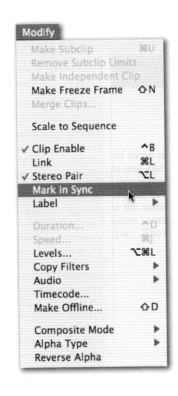

Don't Want to See Red?

Sometimes you want to resync your audio and rid yourself of those red boxes. For example, we were cutting together a thunder and lightning storm and guess what? The claps of thunder didn't match up with the flashes of lighting. (Hey, this is real, and sound travels way slower than light.) Of course, on TV we expect to see and hear these events simultaneously. So what did we do? We unlocked the tracks, slid the audio to match the video, and relocked the tracks. It looked great, except those (now) annoying out-of-sync boxes. There's a simple solution: Highlight the track, and select Modify>Mark in Sync. The red boxes disappear!

48, 44.11, and 32kHz: What's It All About?

Here's the nickel overview of kHz and Final Cut Pro:

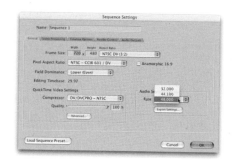

- This is the sampling rate of your audio...higher is better.

- There is a 99-percent probability that you want your sequence to be set to 48kHz.

- Most profession video decks use the 48 kHz standard.

- Music CDs use a standard of 44.1kHz (commonly called the red book standard). You should up-convert these files before importing them into Final Cut Pro. (Final Cut Pro can up convert on the fly, but there's a performance hit.)

- If you set your MiniDV camera to 12 bit (versus 16 bit), you'll be recording at 32kHz.

- Some early MiniDV cameras such as the Sony VX 1000 only record at 32kHz.

- Again, up-convert your files or set your timeline to 32kHz if all of your audio will come from this camera.

- There's a cool new feature in Final Cut Pro 4 that places a green bar inside the top of your audio track (in the timeline) if the audio of the clip doesn't match the sequence audio.

- In Final Cut Pro 4, audio is now rendered at the item level. If you've rendered a rate conversion and move the clip in the timeline, the render file stays attached.

ON THE SPOT

Still Life
Designing and Importing Graphics

Wouldn't it be nice to just be an editor (sigh!) and only have to worry about editing the pictures? You could have a great post team with audio composers, graphic artists, and animators…and, did we mention, you get an assistant editor, too?

Okay, wake up! The days of large post teams with leather couches and fresh-baked chocolate chip cookies are a thing of the past. You have to be able to do it all now. Your client's biggest expectation is good-looking graphics that work.

Don't worry; we've got your back. This chapter presents some great tips on prepping graphics. You'll find all sorts of information about working with Adobe Photoshop and Apple LiveType. We'll unlock the secrets of composite (blending) modes as well as working inside the safe title area. And when you're done, you'll never be afraid of an alpha channel again. As for the fresh baked chocolate chip cookies, we suggest the slice-and-bake variety. Hey, we're all about saving time!

Feel a Change Coming On (Using External Editors)

By using Final Cut Pro's External Editors tab, you can assign Adobe Photoshop (or another graphics application) to be your graphics editor. This allows you greater flexibility in making changes:

❶ Choose Final Cut Pro > System Settings.

❷ Select the External Editors tab.

❸ Click the Set button next to Still Image Files. Select your graphic editor of choice.

❹ Now you can simply contextual-click on a graphic, and choose Open in External Editor.

The graphic will now open into the third-party application. Make any changes, and then close and save your document. As long as you don't add, subtract, or rename layers, the graphic will import correctly and update automatically in the timeline.

> Note: Although you can set an external editor for audio files, it won't work if the audio is part of a video clip.

Gimme Layers

Sometimes you'll want to import a layered Adobe Photoshop file. Final Cut Pro does a good job of this by importing as a composition and turning each layer into a track. To import the PSD file, do one of the following:

● Drag the files or a folder from the finder to a project tab or bin in the Browser.

● Choose Import from the File menu (Command + I). Select File or Folder from the submenu. Select a file or folder in the dialog box, and click Choose.

● Contextual-click in the Browser or a bin's window. Next, choose Import File or Import Folder from the pop-up menu. Select a file or folder; then click Choose.

Didn't I Ask for Layers?

We said Final Cut Pro did a good job of importing PSD files, but it doesn't do a perfect job. There are several features that can't be imported. Why? Well, two different companies make the products, and we're certain neither is fully willing to let all their secrets go.

You must do a little file preparation to make a smooth import. Be sure to work on a duplicate of the original PSD file. The following Adobe Photoshop features are problematic when importing layers:

- Blending Modes (partial support)
- Layer Effects
- Layer/Set mask
- Adjustment Layers
- Grouped layers (layers import, grouping ignored)

Final Cut Pro

Adobe Photoshop 7

When Modes Collide

So you've discovered that some modes work and some do not...bummer. That's okay–you can still work around this limitation. You have two options to solve your problem.

Option 1: Pick a similar mode. Final Cut Pro recognizes most of the "original" blending modes. Subsequent versions of Adobe Photoshop have introduced additional modes. That's okay–they aren't that different.

Adobe Photoshop	Final Cut Pro
Color Burn, Linear Burn	Use Darken or Multiply
Color Dodge, Linear Dodge	Use Lighten or Screen
Vivid Light, Linear Light, Pin Light	Use Hard Light or Overlay
Dissolve, Exclusion, Hue, Saturation, Color, and Luminosity	Must merge layers

Option 2: Merge the blended layers together. Link the two (or more) blended layers together. Choose Merged Linked from the Layers palette submenu.

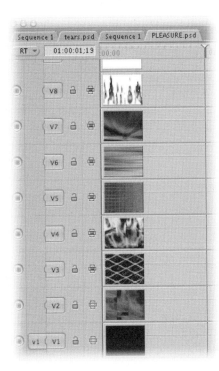

So, What Works?

Final Cut Pro's designers understand that many users will want to bring in layered files for compositing or animation. After all, Final Cut Pro does bill itself as a compositing application, giving users access to many of the commands traditionally associated with Adobe After Effects. Truth be told, about 85 percent of what After Effects imports, Final Cut Pro will bring over. In general, supported features include the following:

- **Layer order and layer name:** Be careful not to change them in your PSD file. Adding and deleting layers after import is also a no-no.

- **Opacity:** The imported layer's opacity becomes the Opacity control in the Motion tab. You can adjust the opacity within Final Cut Pro, as well.

- **Blending Modes:** The following blend modes transfer correctly: Add, Subtract, Difference, Multiply, Screen, Overlay, Hard Light, Soft Light, Darken, and Lighten.

- **Layer group:** Layer grouping is ignored. However, all layers, including grouped layers, import as individual layers.

- **Layer set:** All layers within a layer set are imported to individual layers, but nesting is ignored.

- **Type layers:** Type is rasterized and can't be edited within Final Cut Pro. However, you can switch to Adobe Photoshop via the external editor, and make changes there that will update upon saving.

- **Solid Color Fill layers:** Solid color fill layers are brought in as a graphic with a full-screen, opaque alpha channel.

- **Shape layers:** Shape layers are rasterized and import correctly.

- **Pattern Fill layers:** Pattern fill layers import as the size of the composition.

- **Gradient Fill layers:** Gradient fill layers are preserved upon import.

Mobile Style

Layer Styles (formerly Layer Effects) don't like to travel. This is a common problem because there's not a single application that correctly interprets Layer Styles outside of Adobe Photoshop.

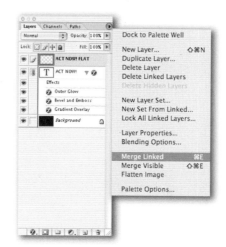

❶   To import successfully, you need to flatten them. Using a technique called Targeted Flattening, you can create a merged layer and preserve an editable layer within the same document. This gives you the best of both worlds: proper imports and room for future revisions. Follow these steps:

❷   Save your document under a different name by using File > Save As. This is an extra precaution against accidentally deleting your work. (We usually rename it **Document Name for FCP.psd**.)

❸   Create a new (empty) layer, and link it to the stylized layer that needs processing. You can link two layers together by clicking in the space between a layers thumbnail and the visibility eyeball.

❹   Leave the empty layer highlighted. While holding down the Option key, choose Merge Linked from the Layers Palette submenu. This merges the layers to the target layer but leaves the originals behind.

❺   You should have a flattened copy on the target layer. Rename this flattened layer so you can easily locate it later. We recommend including the word flat in your layer name for ease of use.

Repeat these steps for all layers, and save your work. This method will produce a layered document, which will import properly into Final Cut Pro.

How to Update a Layer Style

You've imported a layer with a cool layer style applied, and now you need to make changes. If you've followed our advice so far, it's no problem. By using the External Editors tab, you can easily jump back to update a layer. In conjunction with targeted flattening, it's even easier to make changes.

❶ Contextual-click on the graphic in the timeline, and choose Open in Editor.

❷ You'll automatically be switched to Adobe Photoshop if you've set your external editors up correctly.

❸ Select the flattened layer, choose Select All, and press Delete.

❹ Pick the original (unflattened) layer, and make your changes.

❺ Link the editable layer to the "recently" emptied layer. Highlight the Empty layer.

❻ Repeat the targeted flattening procedure by holding down the Option key when you choose Merge Linked.

Close and save your document. When you switch back to Final Cut Pro, your changes will update automatically.

Templates for Menus

Need to create a DVD menu? Use LiveType. What? Use a type program to make a menu? Yup, there are some great templates for DVD menus (as well as bumper graphics) built right in. Simply choose File >Open Template (Shift + Command + O). You can use the Info and Promo categories to create graphics for DVD menus. Simply modify the templates, plug in your video, and change the type – instant motion menu backgrounds to use in iDVD or DVD Studio Pro.

How to Render Less

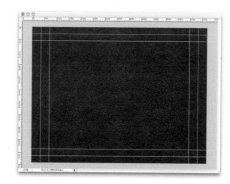

Would you rather render once or 300 times? The answer seems obvious, right? Yet so many people import graphics that are improperly sized into Final Cut Pro. Every graphic that isn't sized properly needs to be rendered.

The solution is to either work in a graphic application that supports non-square pixels or resize before you import. The following chart lists the "native" size your graphics should end up in.

Format	Native Size	Square Pixel Size
601-NTSC 4:3	720x486	720x547
601-NTSC 16:9 Anamorphic	720x486	853x486
DV-NTSC 4:3	720x480	720x540
DV-NTSC 16:9 Anamorphic	720x480	853x480
601/DV-PAL 4:3	720x576	768x576
601/DV-PAL 16:9 Anamorphic	720x576	1024x576

The above are the recommended settings from Apple's Final Cut Pro Group. Several other sources (including the DVD Studio Pro 2 manual) state to use the following measurements. In our experience, both work just fine.

Format	Native Size	Square Pixel Size
601-NTSC 4:3	720x486	720x540
601-NTSC 16:9 Anamorphic	720x486	864x486
DV-NTSC 4:3	720x480	720x534
DV-NTSC 16:9 Anamorphic	720x480	853x480

The best option, though, is to work with a graphics application that supports non-square pixels. This will cut down on your mathematical headaches.

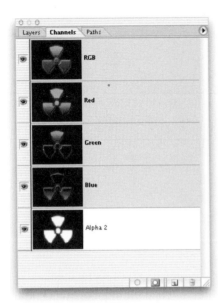

Making an Alpha Channel (One Layer Graphic)

It's very important to get your alpha channel created correctly if you want to "key" a graphic on top of video tracks. An alpha channel contains the transparency of a document saved as the fourth channel in an RGB image. In Final Cut Pro, any area in the alpha channel that's black will allow video to pass through. Alpha channels also allow variable amounts of opacity because shades of gray in an alpha channel show areas of the graphic as partially transparent.

With something so fundamental to video, you'd think there'd be significantly less confusion as to how to create an alpha channel. Here's the fastest way for a single layer document:

1 A perfect alpha channel starts with an active selection loaded. To load a layer, Command + click on the layer's icon in the Layers palette until you see the marching ants. Note: If you have a layer style applied, you must flatten the layer style by merging it with a new empty layer.

2 Switch to the Channels palette, and click the Save Selection As Channel icon.

3 Save your native PSD file. Then pick Save As, and choose to save a PICT file. Make sure the "Alpha Channels" box is checked.

How to Train Your Graphics Department

Graphic editing applications support many color modes. The two you want to use for video work are RGB and Grayscale. Be careful—many stock images and client logos come in the CMYK format. This is designed for print output and will not import correctly into Final Cut Pro. You can check a graphics format by looking at its title bar in Adobe Photoshop.

Making an Alpha Channel (Multiple Layers)

If you have a multilayered document, things are a little trickier. But creating an alpha channel is still an essential part of cleanly keying graphics:

1   Turn off the Visibility icon for all layers that aren't part of the graphic you want to key.

2   Create a new layer, and highlight it.

3   Hold down the Option key and choose Merge Visible from the Layers palette submenu. A new layer is created from the existing layers.

4   Command + click on the layers thumbnail icon to make an active selection. Then turn the visibility icon off for the merged copy.

5   Switch to the Layers palette, and save the selection as a channel.

6   Save your file as a PICT with an alpha channel using the previously described method.

Matte Settings

If you're using glows, drop shadows, or soft edges, you'll likely have a soft edge in your alpha channel. To get the best key possible, you want a clean glow or shadow. But this is difficult if you don't dig deeper into your import graphic settings.

By default, Adobe Photoshop creates a premultiplied alpha channel (an alpha channel that follows the edge exactly). This causes problems, however, because the background color will be visible around the edges of your graphic. If you do nothing, this will be a problem because your glows will look "dirty" and partially transparent drop shadows will come through too strong.

In Final Cut Pro, it's important to identify what the graphic was on top of when the alpha channel was created. If you had a black background, choose Black. If you had a white background or the transparency grid, choose White.

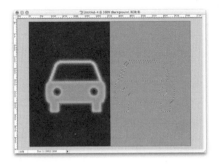

A Better Alpha

For best results, use a straight Alpha channel. In this case, the background color should be the same color as your glow or drop shadow. This way, when the alpha channel is created, the edge has a consistent color (hence it's not premultiplied with a color that must later be removed). This is the preferred method of creating channels, but Adobe Photoshop doesn't work this way. You must place a solid color layer into the background that matches the glow, drop shadow, or soft edge. Note, when creating a straight alpha channel, there's nothing different in the graphic (or fill) area. The essential difference is in the Alpha channel area.

Going to LiveType

Need to bring a logo into LiveType? It's no problem. LiveType recognizes graphics without layers. With this in mind, you can bring in a single-layered PSD file, and it'll see the transparent area around the logo as an alpha channel. For more precision and support of styles, follow the aforementioned advice on creating an alpha channel. Choose Place (Command + I) to import. Using a PICT with alpha channel in RGB mode, you'll be on your way.

Going to LiveType, Part 2

No matter how much it would make your life easier, layered Adobe Photoshop files will not make it into LiveType. It's a good idea to save each layer out as a single graphic. Here's how…the fast way: Adobe Evangelists is a GREAT website to find information about Adobe products such as Photoshop. In the Photoshop area is a collection of Actions. Download the Saving Out Layers action file at http://www.adobeevangelists.com/photoshop/actions.html.

If you're running Photoshop CS, be sure to check out the scripting. You'll find a new script called Export Layers to Files (File>Script> Export Layers to Files) that will do a great job of saving a multilayered document out for import into LiveType.

A Better LiveType

By default, LiveType is likely not configured properly for your system. Be sure to call up Project Properties (Edit >Project Properties), and select the right preset for your tape format. While you're there, be sure to turn Render Fields on for smoother motion. Field rendering will increase your render times, but the quality is worth it. Also, for digital formats, you need to render LOWER field first.

Here's a bonus tip from Steve Martin of Ripple Training: Use Place Background Movie (Shift + Command + I), and bring in a DV file. Check your preferences, and you'll see the project has converted to the aspect ratio of the placed clip.

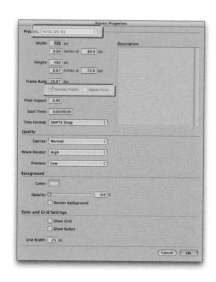

"Free" Backgrounds

LiveType has 168 different textures loaded. They all loop seamlessly, as well. If you're not happy with a default look, you can change the speed as well as the color. You can even get creative by taking a few of them into your Final Cut Pro timeline and mixing them together using composite modes. All of these are royalty free because you've already bought them.

139

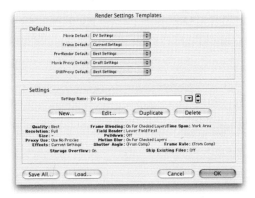

The Right Stuff (Rendering with Presets)

Need to output an Apple QuickTime movie from your motion graphics application? Most other compositing tools also support Output Templates. To get things right every time (without having to think), create templates. Each software package will handle things differently, but the results are the same.

For example, in Adobe After Effects, you can create both Render and Output Templates (Edit>Templates>Render Settings or Output Modules). Use the following settings when designing for NTSC DV video.

Render Settings

Quality	Best
Resolution	Full
Field Render	Lower Field First
Frame Rare	29.97

Output Template

Format	QuickTime Movie
Format Options/Codec	DV/DVCPRO – NTSC
Quality	Best
Channels	RGB
Depth	Millions of Colors
Color	Premultiplied
Audio	48.000kHz
Size	16 Bit
Channels	Stereo

Keyable Movies

Want to create an Apple QuickTime movie that can be keyed through an alpha channel? It's doable if you know what options to pick:

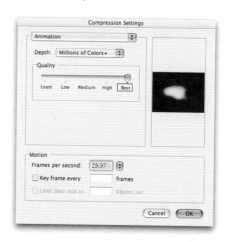

1. Determine if your codec supports embedded alpha channels. Many uncompressed or low compression formats do. If you're using DV however, you must choose Animation.

2. Be sure to choose RGB + Alpha in the Output dialog box if it's an option.

3. Specify Millions of Colors + if you also want to embed an alpha.

4. Render out your file or export it. As long as you've chosen a proper codec and specified to include the alpha, you'll get great results when keying your graphic.

Free Stuff 2

LiveType contains more great things besides textures. You'll find 175 high-quality elements that you can use when creating motion graphics. You can use these in LiveType or export them out for compositing in Final Cut Pro or Adobe After Effects. These animations can serve as transitions or building blocks for your motion graphics work. If you bought similar items from a stock footage company, you could easily pay $2,000 for the collection.

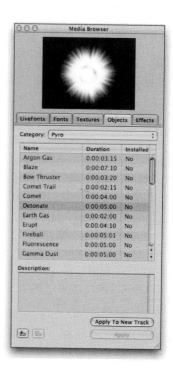

ON THE SPOT

Master of Your Domain
Controlling the Timeline

The sun is shining, and you're driving down the Pacific Coast Highway in a cherry red convertible. You know every bend and curve in the road. Life is good. That's how you should feel about your timeline. It's the window that gets your show from start to finish. The more you know about its nuances, the better your driving experience will be.

In this chapter, we'll show you how to get the most out of your timeline, how to take advantage of its power, and how to do some tricks that will make...well...doing tricks easier.

The timeline in Final Cut Pro has always been flexible. And with Final Cut Pro 4, it has become a contortionist, bending over backward to make your editing life easier. Once you get comfortable with nesting, stacking, resizing, and–well, you get the picture–you'll be the envy of every other driver...um...editor on the road.

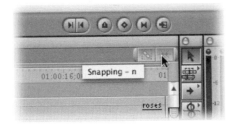

Got Snaps?

Sometimes you want things to quickly jump into their proper place. Final Cut Pro refers to this as snapping. When turned on, items will snap directly to the playhead, an edit point, markers, keyframes, or In and Out points. This makes it easier to align clips (especially when keying graphics on a higher track).

Look for a small gray arrow that appears above or below the point that indicates the item has snapped into place. But what if snapping is getting in the way of your edit or composite? Turn it off!

You can turn snapping on or off at any time, even as you're dragging a clip. Simply press the N key to disable snapping. You'll notice the snapping icon change on the right edge of the Timeline.

Snapping affects several areas besides the Timeline. You may want to turn it off when scrubbing, trimming, or using motion controls. Even the Viewer and the Canvas can be affected.

Tighten Up Your Timeline

A clean tight timeline is a happy Timeline. Here are some quick cleanup tips:

Delete unused tracks: Select Sequence>Delete Tracks. Check both the "Video Tracks" and "Audio Tracks" boxes, and then highlight select "All Empty Tracks."

Drag me down: Reduce your layers. If you have stacked clips upon clips on multiple video tracks, you can hold down the Shift key and drag them to overwrite the clips below them. The Shift key ensures that your clip doesn't move left or right as you move it down.

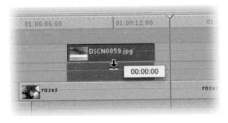

The Dividing Line Part 1

When dragging tracks in the Timeline, where you drag is as important as what you drag. Careless dragging may result in an unintended overwrite edit when you intended an insert edit.

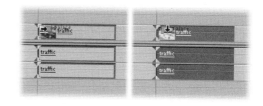

If you look closely at the Timeline, you'll notice that it's divided by a thin gray line. When dragging, look to see which region you enter to determine the edit type.

When dragging from the Viewer or a bin, use these tips:

- Dragging to the upper-third of the track results in an insert edit.

- Dragging to the lower two-thirds of the track results in an overwrite edit.

The Dividing Line, Part 2

Several different options are available when dragging within the Timeline.

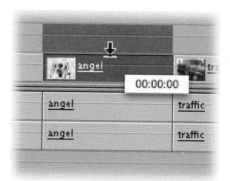

When dragging in the Timeline, use these tips:

- Dragging in the Timeline horizontally results in an overwrite edit by default.

- Dragging in the Timeline horizontally results in an insert or swap edit when you hold down the Option key.

- Dragging in the Timeline vertically results in an overwrite edit by default.

- Dragging in the Timeline vertically results in an insert edit when you press the Option key after you start to drag.

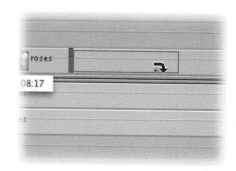

- Pressing the Option key and then dragging in the Timeline vertically results in a cloned copy added to the Timeline via an insert edit.

- Pressing the Option and Shift keys and then dragging in the Timeline vertically results in a cloned copy added to the Timeline directly above the clip.

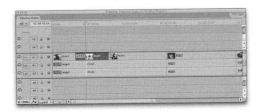

A Little Stability

Tired of scrolling up and down in the Timeline? Need to see audio tracks 1 and 2 so you can mix the music, but there's sound effects and natural sound living on tracks A3–A6? Sometimes it's just hard to see all the tracks you need.

It's easy, however, to create a static region in the middle of the Timeline. The static area can contain video tracks, audio tracks, or both. When you create a static region, you end up with three regions in the Timeline. The top video portion and bottom audio portion are scrollable. The middle portion can be resized and repositioned, but not scrolled. This style of Timeline makes it easy to constantly see your dialogue and A-Roll, while still having access to your other tracks.

To create the static region, drag the thumbtabs to set the number of tracks. Grab the central tab in the static region to move it up and down your Timeline. To eliminate the static region, drag the video tab downward and the audio tab upward.

Don't Drag and Drop

Professional editors edit from the keyboard. Don't believe us? Ever see a concert pianist use a mouse?

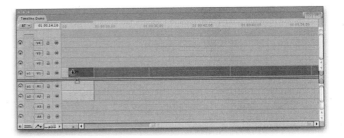

Mute, Solo, Audible: What's the Big Difference?

Here's a distilled overview of Mute, Solo, and Audible and when to use them.

Audible turns a track's sound on and off. If it's off, you can't hear it when you play back from the timeline, and you won't hear it when you print to tape. This is very useful when doing multiple-language programs or news packages where you need version with and without narration. Option + clicking an Audible button leaves that track live and silences all other tracks.

Mute and Solo are opposite sides of the same coin. The Mute button turns off audio playback for that track. The Solo button does the opposite—muting all tracks that don't also have Solo enabled. This is a great way to preview a specific group of audio tracks. Remember that you can mute or solo one or multiple audio tracks.

Note: If you don't see all of these audio controls, be sure to click the Audio Controls button at the bottom of your Timeline.

Use the Solo Item(s) Command

A more advanced solo command is Solo Item(s). Follow these steps:

❶ Select the item(s) you want to solo.

❷ Press Control + S to invoke the Solo Item(s) command.

❸ All non-selected clips (above or below) have their visibility disabled.

❹ Press Control + S to disengage soloed items.

The key advantage to this method is that you'll only lose render files in the soloed and adjacent clips.

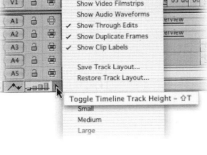

There's a New Triangle in Town

In Final Cut Pro 4 a new drop-down triangle was added to right of the "toggle timeline track height" button. It provides a quick and easy shortcut to several features, such as the following:

- Show Video Filmstrips
- Show Audio Waveforms
- Show Through Edits
- Show Duplicate Frames
- Show Clip Labels
- Save Track Layout
- Restore Track Layout

And it has shortcuts to the four default track heights:

- Reduced
- Small
- Medium
- Large

O, Solo Mio

Have eight layers visible but only want to see one? That's what soloing is for. It's possible to turn off all "other" layers to quickly refine your view. Simply hold down the Option key and click a track's visibility icon. All other tracks are made temporarily invisible. Option + click the soloed track to return to a normal view.

This will affect your render files, so this is most helpful when you're harnessing the power of RT Extreme. Once you get into heavy rendering, try not to turn track visibility on and off, or you'll lose render files.

Let It Roll: Scrolling in the Timeline

Too many tracks in your Timeline, and you want to scroll up and down quickly? No need to grab the scroll bar on the right edge if you have a three-button mouse. Put the cursor over the Timeline, and use the third button to scroll up and down. It gets better; hold down the Shift key and you can scroll left and right. Don't stop now—place the cursor over the viewer or canvas, and you can scrub backward and forward. If you aren't impressed yet by Apple's thoughtful engineers…go try these shortcuts in a bin, on effect sliders, and even in the audio mixer.

Slippin…

Advanced editors know that true power lies in trimming (those minor adjustment made to shots that perfect the edit). Slipping a shot involves changing what portion of the shot is seen while the duration in the Timeline remains constant. Many editors know about the Slip Item tool (S) but don't know about the ability to slip within the viewer. Follow these steps:

❶ Double-click a clip to load it in the viewer.

❷ Hold down the Shift key, and click the In or Out point.

❸ Drag left or right to adjust the shot. The changes update in the Timeline automatically.

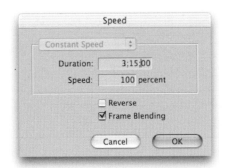

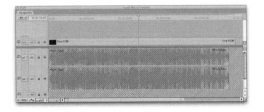

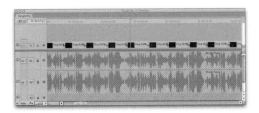

Give Me a Beat: How to Edit to Music

Have you got rhythm? Can you tap to the beat of a song with your foot? How about a finger? If so, you can quickly edit a montage to music:

1 You may want to map the Add Edit command to a single keystroke without a modifier key. You can replace a key you don't use often for this new purpose. If not, the default combo is Ctrl + V.

2 In order to "cut" the beat, you need a solid layer in the Timeline. For this purpose you can use some Slug from the generator menu.

3 Edit the Slug filler into the Timeline on an empty track, and lock all other tracks. Option + click the lock icon for slug track to lock all other video tracks. Be sure to lock the audio tracks, as well.

4 Slug duration is capped at 2:00:00, so you may need change the speed of the slug. Highlight the track, press Command + J, and type in the new duration to match your music track. Changing the speed of the filler doesn't matter because you're going to replace it.

5 Move your cursor to the start of the audio track, and press Play.

6 At each major beat or desired edit point, press the newly assigned key for Add Edit. The filler track will now be chopped up.

7 Filling in the holes is simple. Load the desired source material, and place a single edit point to define the In or Out point.

8 In the Timeline, press the X key to mark your In and Out point.

9 Press F10 to perform an Overwrite edit.

10 Repeat steps 7 and 8 until the end of the Slug is reached.

Close the Gap

This trick is particularly helpful when cutting down long interviews or closing gaps in a sound bite. When you find an area that needs to be exorcized, you can quickly make the cut from the keyboard (without having to switch tools). Simply load the entire clip into the Timeline, and then edit it down on the fly. Follow these steps:

❶ When you hit the first gap, press I to mark an In point.

❷ When you hit the end of the gap, press O to mark an Out point.

❸ Press the Forward Delete key. On a PowerBook, press Shift + Delete.

❹ Resume playing, and repeat the procedure for the next gap.

Close Those Tabs

So you want to close those 27 open sequences in your Timeline? Well, you can do them one at a time...drag...click...drag...click...drag...you get the point. Or, you could just option + W the whole window...wait, that doesn't work. All the sequences are still there the next time you open the Timeline.

Here a couple of quick solutions: If you want to keep just one sequence open, drag its tab off the Timeline, and then close the other Timeline with the 26 open sequences. If you want to close all the sequences and not have them there the next time you open your Timeline, simply press Command + W with the Canvas window selected.

Nest Be Gone

In the old days (pre-June 2003), if you dragged one sequence from your browser into another sequence in your Timeline, you'd simply have the nested sequence in your Timeline. Not always what you wanted.

Now if you hold down the Command key while dragging the sequence into the Canvas or Timeline, all the individual clips will appear in your Timeline exactly as they appear in nested sequence from which they're sourced.

If you hold the Command key while dragging to the Timeline, Final Cut Pro will automatically add the needed tracks. If you're going to drag to the Canvas, however, it's very important to make sure you have enough tracks in your destination Timeline; otherwise only some of the tracks will come over.

Fly!

It's possible to trim on the fly. This way you can listen for an audio edit or look for a particular visual cue.

Enter trim mode, and press the space bar to cycle your trim.

When you reach the desired edit point, press the I key to move your In point.

Press the up or down arrow to move through the Timeline to your next edit point.

Zoom...Zoom

Want to see the entire Timeline from start to finish? Press Shift + Z to make the entire Timeline to Fit to Window. On the other hand, want to zoom in on just the selected area? Highlight one or more clip, and press Shift + Option + Z to Fit to Selection. These are valuable buttons that you should map to your Timeline window's button bar.

Where Do You Trim?

Sometimes you'll want to trim the incoming or outgoing side of an edit point. Instead of having to switch tools or hold down a modifier key, simply tap the U key. This will cycle your trim from centered at cut to incoming to outgoing.

ON THE SPOT

CHAPTER

Crisis Management
Troubleshooting and Recovery Techniques

It's always darkest just before it goes completely black. That's how it feels as your deadline approaches and your system starts to act up. Clients are waiting, the FedEx guy has his feet up on your desk drinking his second cup of coffee, and if you're really quiet you can actually hear the gremlins laughing.

Most of the time, it only takes a few tricks to crush the gremlins and get your project out the door. This chapter will help you troubleshoot what's going wrong and provide tips for fixing it. (The odds are that it's between 3 and 5 a.m. when you're reading this, and there's no one to call who won't hang up on you.)

Take a deep breath, and slowly read this chapter's tips. Sometimes the light at the end of the tunnel isn't another oncoming train; sometimes it's really your show getting put to tape.

Test It

If you think you have a problem, you need to isolate the problem and test it thoroughly. By taking the time to gather the right information, you'll make it easier for others to help you. Answer these questions:

● What are the symptoms of the problem?

● When does the problem appear?

● Is the problem specific to one machine, or does it repeat on several machines?

● When did the problem start happening? Have you installed any software lately?

● Is it a video-only problem? Audio only?

● Can you replicate the problem consistently?

Delete Preferences

Deleting preferences files often solves system and application quirkiness. But where are they, and which ones do you delete? If you discovered that everything works fine when you create a new user (see the earlier tip), then go into your Home folder>Library>Preferences>Final Cut Pro User Data and delete the Final Cut Pro Preferences configuration file.

It rebuilt the next time you restart the application.

If things are still cranky, you may want to trash the com.apple.FinalCutPro.plist file, which you can find in the Preferences folder.

When in Doubt, Shut Down and Restart

Things can and do go wrong. A simple reset to your system is often the best way to "cure" software problems. Don't just click Restart, however; let the system fully reset itself by shutting down. As a favorite engineer used to tell me, "Shut down, count to 20, restart...if there's still a problem, then call me."

Remove Third-Party Preferences

Okay, just because you can put a plug-in in the Plugins folders doesn't mean you should. We know someone who successfully put their U.S. hairdryer into an overseas socket...well, 220 volts later their hairdryer and their arm was still tingling. So if your problems started after you installed or activated a third-party plug-in, try removing it and seeing if that removes the problem.

Note: Although many Adobe After Effects plug-ins work inside of Final Cut Pro, not all do. Also, several manufacturers have different versions to install into Final Cut Pro. Be sure to check your install disc or the manufacturer's website for details.

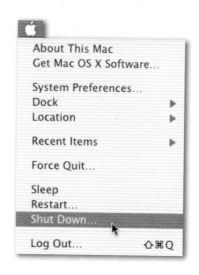

Unexpected Quits

Okay, this may seem obvious to some of you. Make sure you have the latest "blessed" versions of Final Cut Pro, Apple QuickTime, the OSoperating system, and any third-party drivers required for your system (AJA, Pinnacle, and so on). By "blessed," we mean the versions and combinations that Apple lists on its website. Go to www.finalcutpro.com, and click Support. We had a client complain about Final Cut Pro's stability on a beta of the operating system and of QuickTime. Yes, they were public betas, but that doesn't mean you have to install them.

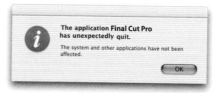

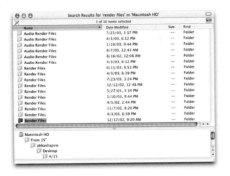

'I Can't Even Open My Project File' (Or Other Flaky Activities)

Corruption can happen a lot of places...even in Final Cut Pro. Here are some steps to take if your project quits on opening:

❶ Look in the Autosave Vault. Before panicking, simply try going back a few versions. Do a search for Autosave in the Finder. Look in the folders for a backup of your project file. Work your way backward through the recently saved copies.

❷ Create a new user account. Create a new user account for testing purposes. This is a great way to see if the problem is a corrupt preferences file. Most Final Cut Pro preferences files are stored in the user's settings. Open the System Preferences panel under the blue apple. Click Accounts. Click on new user. Create one call test, and give it admin privileges. You can assign it a password or not. Only use this account for troubleshooting (you may want to keep it for the future).

Now, log out (again under the blue Apple), and long in as the new user. Try opening Final Cut Pro. It should open with no active project files. If it opens, you've narrowed the problem down to bad user preferences (see next tip) or a bad project file.

❸ Test the project file. Next, open the project file that was causing the problems. (If it was stored in the other user folder, you won't have access to it. Log in as the original user, make a copy of the file, and move it to a shared location such as the media folder or the top level of your hard drive–not the desktop...that's owned by the user.)

If it opens, you've confirmed it was the preferences. If it crashes, it could be bad media or renders, or something has become corrupt in the application or the operating system.

❹ Delete the render files. Delete all the render files. Don't worry–you can rerender a lost faster than you can rebuild the project. To find render files, look on your media drives for the Render Files and Audio Render Files folders. Terminate them with extreme prejudice. Yes, it's Apocalypse Now for your render files.

Try reopening the project. Success? If not, try hiding the media files from the project. Disconnect the media drive, or drop the media into another folder. If the project opens with the media offline, you've got a bad media file. (An alternative is to open the project file on another machine...same rules apply.)

❺ **Recapture the media.** If you determine you have a bad file, you can either load/relink media back into the project in small groups or batch recapture the media from the original tapes.

If you're still getting tanked, send the project to a friend to see if it'll open on their machine. This is the best way to determine if you're having a hardware, application, or operating system issue.

❻ **Still broken?** At this point, you may need to call your reseller or a consultant.

Disable Extensions

In the "old days," you'd turn off your extensions when booting, but OS X doesn't have extensions, right? Well, actually it does, and you can boot into Safe Boot/Safe Mode to see if the problem is caused by a non-Apple extension:

❶ Shut down your Mac all the way. (Choose Shutdown from the Apple menu, not Restart.)

❷ Press the power button, and wait for the chime.

❸ Immediately after the chime, press and hold the Shift key. When the gray apple and spinning gears show up, let go.

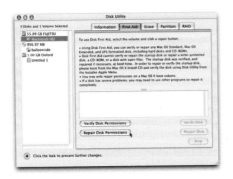

Rebuilding Permissions

This sounds like something from etiquette class, but this little activity can save hours of headache throughout your systems. In the Utilities folder in the Applications folder, there's an application called Disk Utility. Under the First Aid tab, there's a button to repair permissions (Repair Disk Permissions). Select your drives, and let it rip. You should run it a couple of times. It's amazing how so many of those little quirky problems will go away.

Zap the PRAM

We like this tip because it separates the geeks from the uber-geeks. PRAM is the Parameter RAM, which is an area of RAM that's used to store information about your computer. It stores things such as startup device, date, time, time zone, mouse speed, and the like.

If the information in the PRAM becomes corrupted, odd and spooky things can occur; you can clear the information and reset it to factory settings.

To reset PRAM, follow these steps:

❶ Restart your computer while pressing Command + Option + P + R.

❷ As the computer begins to restart, you'll hear the startup chime repeat. Continue pressing the keys until the chime has sounded three or more times.

❸ Release the keys, and the startup should complete.

You should feel rather wizardly by now.

True Uber-Geekdom: FSCK

If you're having system problems and want to clean the disk, check partitions, and so on, here's a way to fix problems without any third-party applications: Start up in single-user mode, and run FSCK…uh, what was that?

FSCK – fsck stands for "file system check," and the -y you'll type just says to go ahead and fix any problems it finds.

Here's the drill….

❶ Restart your Mac.

❷ Immediately press and hold Command + S. You'll see a bunch of text begin scrolling on your screen. (Cool, you're now a geek.) Soon you'll see the Unix command line prompt (#). Don't cry; it's still your Mac—you're just a true Unix god…well, pre-god.

Now that you're at the # prompt, here's how to run FSCK:

❶ Type **fsck -y** (that's fsck + space + minus+ y).

❷ Press Return.

The FSCK utility will do its magic, running some text across your screen. If there's damage to your disk, you'll see a message that says: "FILE SYSTEM WAS MODIFIED."

If you see this message, it found some problems and fixed them—repeat steps 1 and 2 until that message no longer appears. It's normal to have to run FSCK more than once; the first run's repairs often uncover additional problems.

When FSCK finally reports that no problems were found and the # prompt reappears, type **reboot** to restart or type **exit** to start without rebooting. Then press Return.

Your Mac should proceed to start up normally to the login window or the Finder.

Get More Help

Yes, we know you can find it in the Help menu, but these are killer startup shortcuts for OS X that we never can remember–so here they are, straight from the Help menu.

Start up from a CD: Hold down the C key on startup.

Eject CD on startup (which is great if you're stuck in an endless boot to the CD system folder: Hold down the mouse button on startup.

Select a startup disk (on some computers): Hold down the Option key. You'll see all disks that have bootable system drives.

Prevent startup items from opening (great for troubleshooting): Press the Shift key.

Prevent automatic login (if you want to start up from a different user, even though you have auto login turned on): Hold down the left Shift key and the mouse button when you see the progress bar.

Close open Finder windows: Press the Shift key.

Reset Parameter RAM: Press Command + Option + P + R.

Show console messages (verbose mode). This makes you look really knowledgeable and freaks out other Mac users: Press Command + V.

Start up using Mac OS X rather than Mac OS 9: Press Command + X.

And, of course, if you have a frozen Mac (we're talking spinning beach ball of death, ice-age frozen): Hold down the power button for several seconds and several seconds more…until it reboots.

Make Sure You're Getting the Right Help

If you upgraded from version 2 or 3 to version 4, the Help system has changed. Earlier versions of Final Cut Pro used the Help Center, but version 4 switched to a PDF document. The problem? Your version 3 Help files are still loaded, and the information there is wrong.

So know which version of Help files you're looking at. Finding Help within the application opens the right docs, but if you open the Help from the Finder-level Help pull-down menu (Command + ?), you get the Help files for previous versions of Final Cut Pro that are installed in your Applications folder.

The trick to know is that Help files are located in the application's package. Once you can fully migrate to version 4, simply throw away the version 3 or earlier application package—the old Help files are gone, and you can rip this page out for the book. (Just don't lend it to anyone still using version 3 on their system.)

Dropped FireWire Frames—Not Really

Say you're dropping frames right off the bat...every time you try to capture. This is not a problem. Depending on your FireWire drive, bridgeboard, and computer, you may always drop the first frame of video on every capture. Don't worry; everything catches up 1/30 of a second later. Just capture an extra one-second handle, and turn off the "abort on capture on dropped frames" option in the User Preferences window. And go, go, go....

Just to make sure that the only place you're dropping frames is the first frame, highlight the captured clip(s) in your Browser, and select Tools>Long Frames>Mark. You should se a little yellow marker at the beginning of the shot—and only there. If you have long frame markers in other places, see the next few tips.

Real Dropped Frames Solutions

Follow these steps if you're really dropping frames:

1 Check your cable (not the one that gives you HBO and CNN—your FireWire cable). A quick swap or even replugging in the cable could solve the problem.

2 What's the bridgeboard on your FireWire enclosure? Currently there are three flavors of bridgeboards inside of FireWire enclosures that convert your IDE drives to FireWire drives: Oxford 900, Oxford 911, and 922 (FireWire 800). If your enclosure uses an old 900 board, your throughput could be compromised. (It's 1/3 the speed of the 911 boards.) If you have a 922 board, you should be the envy of all your friends...unless you're using an old computer that doesn't have a FireWire 800 port. Don't worry—you can get an adapter for your old FireWire cable or, better yet, put in a FireWire 800 PCI card.

3 You should try swapping the chain. If your camera is plugged into a drive, try plugging it into a separate port (or, better yet, separate card). If you're dropping frames and the camera is on a separate chain, place it at the end of a drive chain. Different manufacturers prefer different cabling practices.

4 If you're still dropping frames, it could be an OS problem or preferences issue. Try updating Apple QuickTime, and check out the other appropriate troubleshooting tips in this chapter.

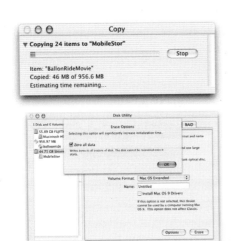

Media with a Mind of Its Own

Sometimes if you're having problems with a file or files, it's because your hard drive may be going south. Try moving your media files to another drive or even to an internal one if you're using an external drive. A low-level reformat on the flaky drive will block out bad sectors. Warning: This WILL ERASE all media on that drive. If a drive starts acting finicky, toss it—your time is worth more than 120GB of lost data. Drives are cheap; your time isn't!

90 Percent Of Problems Are Cable Problems

Most people assume the worst when their edit system starts acting up. If you're getting a signal or device control problem, it might not be your machine (or even your software). A $10 cable can tear down an entire edit session. Follow these steps:

❶ Shut down the computer to avoid any improper dismounting of media drives.

❷ Isolate the suspected problem device.

❸ Be sure to reseat both ends of the cable.

❹ If that doesn't work, try swapping out the cable.

❺ Continue to add devices until the problem recurs. Then repeat this cycle.

You might be surprised how many times this works.

Remember, there's more than just FireWire cables; there are USB cables, RS-422 cables, monitor cables and extensions, and fiber-optic cables. Even your audio and video cables (RCA, BNC, XLR) could be culprits. "What, no video? Oops, my RCA came unplugged."

Contain Yourself

If you're having problems putting your project to tape because of dropped frames or crashes, try creating a Self-Contained Movie file, dropt it into a new sequences, and use sequences to print/edit to video. Yes, this will eat up a lot of disk space, but it may be the only way to get that opus out to your client.

Camera's Gone Wild

If you're having problems controlling your DV camera or deck, you may want to switch your camera/deck control to FireWire basic. If your device is still acting unruly, the Extras folder on your Final Cut Pro install disc contains some additional plug-in files (DV tuners) that must be installed on your computer if you're using certain DV devices. Go to Apple's Final Cut Pro site at www.finalcutpro.com to see if your device requires a plug-in.

Wrong Sequence Presets = Red Bars

If every time you add a clip to your Timeline, you see red (bars, that is), chances are your Sequence Settings are wrong. You can change the Active Sequence settings by pressing Command + 0, then clicking the Load Sequence Preset button, and selecting the proper settings. You may also simply choose to copy and paste the clips to a properly sized sequence.

For future use, it's a good idea to set these settings when you create the sequence. Under User Preferences, choose "Prompt for settings on New Sequence."

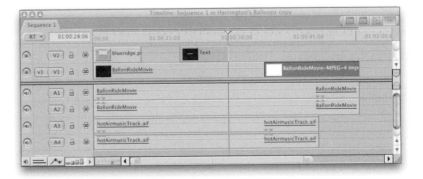

Photo Credit Blue Ridge Balloon Company

Is It Fresh? (Check for Updates)

Companies can't test every scenario that someone might use their software in. This is why there are "dot" releases. Oftentimes minor bugs are fixed, or you can get better compatibility with newer versions of the operating system or QuickTime in the free updates. Sometimes they'll even add features.

There's a new updater that you can automatically download into your software updater panel, called Pro Application Support. If you install this updater, you'll be notified whenever any of your Apple Pro apps have been enhances with a "dot" release.

Lost Window Part 1- No Canvas

As obvious as this one is, we get calls almost weekly with folks calling up and telling us that the app is broken because all they see is their Browser and their Viewer windows. The others are gone. This is a simple fix that we'll keep between us: You have no sequences open. Open any sequence from your Browser, and–Boom!–there are your Canvas and Timeline windows.

Stuttering Video

If your video playback is jerky in your Canvas or Viewer, you may need to adjust your view settings. Click the zoom pop-up menu and select Fit to Window, or press Shift + Z. You should set both the Viewer and Canvas to this setting, especially if you frequently change window layouts. This way the video size will scale to match the window and give you the smoothest playback.

My Render Files are Gone

If they're really gone, don't worry—you can always rerender. However, usually lost render files are a case of, "I've targeted my render file location under System Settings>Scratch Disk tab to a drive that's no longer attached to my machine." If this is the case, plug it in and link the lost render files back to the project.

Another option is that the folder containing the reference files could've been moved. To find all the reference files on your hard drives, do a search in the Finder for the render files and Kind folder...you'll be amazed at what you'll find.

By the way, this is a great way to clean house and get back some lost hard drive space.

What's That Exclamation Point?

A lot of new users and users new to version 3 and 4 of the application call us up asking about that exclamation point or nice green check mark on their image. We tell them that Final Cut Pro has an Artificial Intelligence engine, and it's approving of the shot or edit. Or, if there is an exclamation point, then there's content that's inappropriate for people younger than 18. They thank us and hang up the phone.

After about five minutes, they call us back and ask if we were pulling their legs. Well, Final Cut Pro does have a secret AI engine...if we told you more, we'd be put on double-secret probation...but the exclamation point and checkbox actually mean something else.

They're used to determine if your video is broadcast safe/legal. An exclamation point means you're not broadcast safe, and a green checkbox or one with an up arrow means you're okay. Now how did this get turned on? Well, the keyboard shortcut for this is Control + Z, so people often accidentally hit it when trying to do an undo (Command + Z) or a fit to window (Shift + Z).

Where's My Image?

This one happens all the time. "My video is gone…my video is gone!" There's a good change you've slipped into one of the wireframe modes used for fast previews of motion graphics. Simply highlight the Viewer or Canvas that's affected, and press the W key until the picture returns.

Photo Credit Blue Ridge Balloon Company

Lost Window, Part 3: Hidden Windows

Being fans of keyboard shortcuts, we love to use Command + 1–6 to toggle which window is active. However, if a window is already active and you use its keyboard shortcut, it actually hides the window. (You can also create this problem by cycling and unchecking these windows in the Window pull-down.)

The solution again is easy: Either reuse the shortcut, revealing the window, or go to the Window menu pull-down, and check the appropriate "hidden" window.

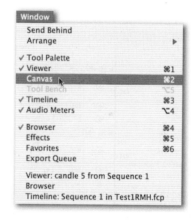

Can't Add a Dissolve

When creating a transition between clips, you're essentially overlapping the two clips. If you've set your In and Out points to close to the end of the clip, you won't have enough space for the transitions to occur. You can use the Slip tool to adjust the shot so there's more overlap. For future edits and logging, it's a good rule of thumb to allow at least one-second "handles" beyond your marks.

Number Lock

PowerBook users beware: This one gets even us some of the time. If you look on the right side of your keyboard, you'll notice that there are small numbers on some of the keys. This is essentially a numeric keypad. How do you access it? Simple—you just push the Num Lock key if you want a numeric keypad (just like the ones on a full-size keyboard). This sounds convenient until you accidentally push the Num Lock key, which is right next to your Volume Up key. Let's just say panic ensues when you can't log in to your PowerBook and only a third of the keys seem to work. Be sure to check the Num Lock key, and see if it's lit up. Chances are you want this "feature" off.

Win the Battle of the Pre-Roll

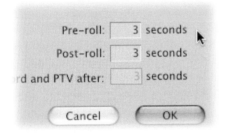

If you're trying to batch capture and your system keeps aborting because of "not enough pre-roll," You can go into the Audio/Video Preferences settings and go to the Device Control Presets to create a new preset and reduce the amount of pre-roll needed to capture. Remember, some decks have minimum pre-roll requirements. In this case, use the Capture Now setting, and you be the pre-roll button. If you're still hitting a "can't capture" wall, dub the tape onto another tape with existing control track at the head of the shot.

Lost Window, Part 2: Minimize

OS X has a great feature called Minimize. It hides any open window in the Dock. Unfortunately, a lot of folks hit this one by accident and "lose" one of their key editing windows. So look in your Dock, and see if any of those lost windows are just hanging out waiting to be found.

The hack WindowShade X lets you convert this button to allow you to roll up your window or minimize in place. Better yet, the haxie allows you to disable the Minimize feature entirely just within Final Cut Pro. This is a great solution until Apple restores this feature in a future OS.

Where Has My Audio Gone?

See your picture, but can't hear it? You may need to check several things:

1 Is the computer volume turned up? (We had to ask.)

2 Are the speakers are powered and connected? (We had to ask that, too.)

3 Check View>External Video, and be sure it is set to off. By the way, you can create a button and a keyboard shortcut that will turn external video off in Final Cut Pro 4.

4 Check your Audio/Video Settings, and set Audio Playback to the "Built-in audio controller."

What's That Beeping Sound?

When you play your Timeline, do you hear a loud series of beeps? This is your clue that you have run out of RAM to preview your unrendered audio tracks (or your microwave dinner is ready).

Remember, you may think you're only using six or eight audio tracks, but if you mix sample rates, add filters, or even have cross dissolves between tracks, Final Cut Pro sees may see those six to eight tracks as 20–24 tracks. The result is you're more likely to "break" real-time previews. Follow these steps:

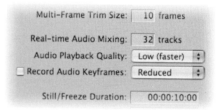

1 You can increase the number of tracks set in your User Preferences. Simply put a higher number in the "Real-time Audio Mixing" box. Eight was the default for way back in Final Cut Pro 1.0 (which ran on a G3), so chances are you can up that to 16, 32, or even 64 (and that "new" G7 25GHz machine will surely play all 99 tracks).

2 Render. Audio renders are usually quick and free up memory for your cool eight-track quad-split with color-correction cross-wipe transitions.

Help...My Video Looks Like a Badly Dubbed Foreign Movie

Lip-flap is acceptable in poorly dubbed Hong Kong martial arts films but not to most of your clients. If you're using Final Cut Pro 3.04 or earlier, there's a "Sync Adjust after X minutes" setting in the User Preferences panel. The default checkbox is set to On. Guess what? Most of you need to uncheck this box, or you'll actually throw your audio OUT OF SYNC. This setting is to compensate for the early Cannon XL-1 cameras, which drifted a bit on long captures. Double-check Apple's Final Cut Pro website, but odds are that you need to turn this off.

Help...My Sync, Part 2

In Final Cut Pro 4, this is no longer an issue because this checkbox is gone. Hallelujah.

Here's some good news: You've captured 29 hours of footage with the sync audio adjust on and now it all drifts. With tears in your eyes, you're ready to recapture all 29 hours, which reside on 127 tapes. Fear not...here's a five-minute solution if you're working with version 3 of the application.

The audio sync compensation happens when the clip is brought into the Browser.

Simply delete all copies of these clips from your Browser, turn off the "Sync Adjust" checkbox, and drag the already captured clips back into the Browser.

Life is once again good.

"But I'm Not Trying to Make a Silent Movie!"

You've captured all your clips without audio, and you can't change the capture settings (or some variation of that). What do you do? Many times we've had clients call us up saying that they just finished the world's largest batch capture but used the wrong capture settings and forgot to capture audio. They didn't panic until they realized that when they went into the Browser to modify the clips settings (which you can do in large numbers by just Command + clicking multiple clips), they couldn't change it from video only. No matter how hard they tried, cried, and lied ("I did have the right settings...it must be a bug!"*), they couldn't change the settings in the Browser. They call us hoping for a solution other than "tough bananas, you're going to have to relog everything" or some convoluted batch list export and import dance.

Fear not. The secret is to throw away the original clips or simply Control + click, and make the clips Offline. Switch to List view and now you can change the capture options and rebatch.

> * By the way, we don't believe in bugs, just undocumented features.

Buttons Get the Right Mix

Want to switch your audio performance settings? You can quickly switch between Real-time Audio Mixing through buttons. The Button List allows you to map buttons for Real-time Audio Mixing to any button bar. You can choose from 8, 12, 16, 32, 64, and 99 tracks. You'll probably want to stay away from the higher track settings unless you have an abundance of RAM to spare.

Learn All About Hard Drives and Storage

You can never have too much or too fast when it comes to storage solutions for video. The use of DV-25 video has allowed a large number of people (users) to become complacent about storage because of the way FireWire has been implemented. You should learn a few tricks about hard drives so that you'll have some hair remaining on your head after you edit.

More storage is better, and you never now how much you need until you run out. Also remember that renders and alternative versions require disk space, too. Leave approximately 15 to 20 percent of the available drive space as overhead. This will to allow you to render files, to make DVDs for archiving, and to play back without disk errors. If you render a 30 minute show with a time code burn or a widescreen matte…you're going to create a 6 gb file in DV and 30 gb file in SD!

Data Rates for Video (and Audio)

The following are the data rates for video (and audio):

OfflineRT (using Photo JPEG)	Between 300–500KB/sec.
DV-25	3.75MB/sec.
DVCPRO-50	7.6MB/sec.
2:1 compressed M-JPEG	14MB/sec.
Uncompressed 8-bit standard definition video	27MB/sec. (SDI)
Uncompressed 10-bit SD video with alpha	34MB/sec.
Uncompressed 8-bit 1080i HD video	121.5MB/sec.
Uncompressed 10-bit 1080i HD video	182.3MB/sec.

Maximum Data Transfer Rates for Different Types of Hard Drives

The following are the maximum data transfer rates for different types of hard drives:

- FireWire 400 has a maximum data rate of 40Mbps, but the reality is closer to 6–10Mbps.

- FireWire 800 has a data rate of 80Mbps, but the reality is closer to 16–28Mbps.

- SCSI-3 has data rates of 40MBps and is called Ultra Wide SCSI.

- The 160 SCSI Low Voltage Differential (LVD) data rate is 160Gbps.

- The 320 SCSI LVD data rate is 320Gbps.

SCSI data rates are described as the rate at the bus, not what the drives can or will actually handle. For instance, 160 SCSI means that the {Theoretical} data rate tops out at 160Mbps. but this isn't possible in reality do to the need for the drive to communicate sector position, data mapping, write a directory, and then update all of the information back to the host machine. The best you can do for a data rate is 135Mbps with 12-15,000rpm drives on 4 separate 160 SCSI buses with the drives striped into a single volume. The LVD allows for 2–5 times longer cable lengths than traditional SCSI cabling..

Data rates for drives are often expressed as megabits per second (Mbps) or gigabits per second (Gbps) of actual data. This is a misnomer to the average user because the data rate sustained by a drive has a number of factors that relate to speed. How fast the drive spins, how it was formatted, the amount of data on the disk, the number of disks the data is being written across, and even the drive manufacturer all affect the speed at which drives handle data. Other factors also affect how fast the machines run, background actions, faxing, surfing the Internet; these all pull CPU cycles that are needed when creating video.

Gary Adcock, Studio 37, Founder and President of the Chicago FCP User Group

ON THE SPOT

The Finish Line
Learning Advanced Finishing Techniques

Spit and polish! That's the difference between an average show and one that shines to your client. You've slaved over the creation of your opus and are ready to take it to the world. Often it's the last 5 percent of effort that elevates your show and your editing skills from the rest of the pack.

It's all in the details. Are your video levels legal, is your audio balanced, do your renders need rendering? We took you up to the finish line; in this chapter, we'll show you how to cross it with style.

In this race, it's best to take a break before your sprint into the home stretch. A rested editor with some time and distance will see mistakes that an exhausted editor will miss after the 22nd hour of editing. So take a time-out. Go get yet another cup of coffee, watch a cartoon, take five, listen to Take Five (every good editor should know classic jazz), and come back to your show with fresh eyes.

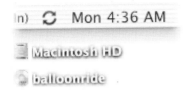

Little Things

When finishing a show, it's the little things that make all the difference. The difference between good and great can be as small as 5 percent. If at all possible, never finish a show at the end of your shift. After several weeks (or even months) of work put into the average project, it's worth tackling it fresh in the morning.

Check for Flash Frames

Before we print to tape, we step through our finished shows one edit at a time, just to make sure we don't have any black flash frames. Use the up and down arrow keys to take you from edit point to edit point. If your canvas shows a black frame (or unintentional frame), you have a flash frame. Switch to trimming, and you can take the offending frames out.

Bad Dissolves

It's very easy to get flash frames in transitions. They can be caused by a shot change at the end of your clip. This happens a lot when editing together previously cut material. It's not your fault really; you can't always know that a transition will use parts of the clip you couldn't see when you started the edit.

Photo Credit Blue Ridge Balloon Company

❶ The easiest way to check is to enter trim mode. Double-click an edit to enter trim mode. You need to be right on the cut or just let your fingers do the work by pressing Option + 7.

❷ Press the space bar to review the edit. Watch it closely looking for a scene change midtransition. Often a one- or two-frame roll edit will solve the problem and not change the feel of the show.

❸ Press the down arrow to move to the next edit or the up arrow to move to the previous edit.

Learn to Cut with L-Cuts

Experienced editors know that changing picture and sound at the same point (a straight cut) can be very jarring. It's more noticeable when both elements change suddenly, which can be jarring to the viewer. A much better method is to try and use an L-cut (so called because of its shape in the Timeline). In this case, the picture edit happens before or after the edit.

These are especially helpful when editing dialogue because they give the editor better control over pacing and reaction shots. You can also use an L-cut to hide a continuity error. Although the difference may sound small, you'll soon discover what an impact they have on a professional edit. Follow these steps:

Photo Credit Blue Ridge Balloon Company

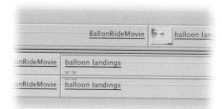

❶   Move through your Timeline, and select edit points with the rolling edit tool.

❷   Double-click to enter trim mode.

Use the comma (,) and period (.) keys to make minor one-frame edits. Better yet, click the dynamic trimming box, and you can use the J-K-L keys to quickly trim your show.

Don't Get Bored When Choosing Transitions

Don't let bad transitions happen to good sequences. We often see editors get "bored" by a show because they've spent too much time on it. They lose any sense of judgment and resort to using "one of everything" from the Transitions menu.

Constrain yourself when using wipes. A few wipes go a long way. Transitions should only be used when needed to show a change in space or time. It's also a good idea to follow a directional transition with an identical transition in the opposite direction. As a cinema classic once said, "Wax on…wax off."

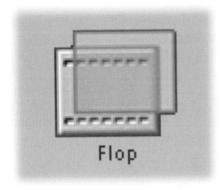

Flop

Visual Contrast

While watching your show, are you noticing that almost every person in it is looking in the same direction? This seems to happen a lot unless producers and DPs pay conscious effort to screen direction. Sometimes, this is beyond their control because several different sources may be used to build a show.

Don't worry; a simple built-in effect can save you. Use the Flop filter to reverse screen direction (Effects> Video Filters> Perspective> Flop). You don't need to maintain a L-R-L-R-L-R visual order throughout, but try to get some visual intercutting by changing the direction your subject looks.

Be careful not to flop a screen with text elements or a clock in it. Also try to keep someone looking the same way throughout the piece.

The Best Part Is No Part At All

Some shots flop better than others. People often notice if hair is suddenly parted on the "wrong" side. Try to choose your flop wisely. No part, center part, or follicly challenged interviewees work the best. Remember shirt pockets and little alligators. Polo players wearing little alligators tend to have them on the left side of a shirt...and just because you can't read it doesn't mean that your audience can't!

Photo credit James Ball

Veja Dupe

Ever get that feeling like you've seen a shot before? It's easy to lose track of every shot cut into your show. It's an unintentional gaffe to repeat a shot in a show unless it's for special storytelling purposes. But how can you find those sneaky dupes?

Don't worry; Final Cut Pro 4 makes it easy:

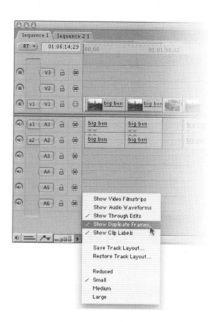

❶ Check your Dupe Detection settings. Press Option + Q to call up your User Preferences panel. Unless you're working in film when you should use at least one frame of handle, you can set the threshold up to 15 frames.

❷ Open Sequence | Sequence Settings (Command + 0), select the Timeline tab, and specify Show Duplicate Frames. You can also access this more quickly from the Track Layout menu at the bottom of the Timeline.

❸ Six different colors are used to mark duplicated frames: red, green, blue, white, black, and purple. Final Cut Pro will mark the duplicate frames along the bottom edge of a clip in the Timeline. If you have more than six duplicated clips, the colors are reused. If a duplicate clip has a motion effect applied, duplicate frame indicators will not appear.

❹ You can contextual-click a clip with duplicate frames to see a shortcut menu. One of the options is Duplicate Frames. It'll show you a list of all repeated clips and indicate how many frames were repeated.

❺ You can choose an item from the list, and the playhead will jump to that point of your sequence. This way you can review each shot and decided if changes are needed.

Delete Unused Tracks

Under the Sequence menu, there's an option to delete unused audio and video tracks...use it!

Jamming Out in the Edit Suite

We've had online sessions where getting the audio mix finalized was virtually impossible—not because of the material but rather because the client and producer just kept talking about where to order lunch. As we turned the volume up to hear better, they just kept talking louder. Finally, they asked us to turn the speakers down…at which point we pointed out that we were happy to go take a break and return when we could finish our audio edit.

My more recent solution is to block the noise out. Although you might look funny to others in your office, a good pair of studio monitoring headphones goes a long way. Block out the environmental noise, and focus on your audio edit. Plus you'll no longer have to worry about your client's habit of talking on their cell phone during the session.

We also like some of the new high-end noise-canceling headsets. They filter out all of the machine hum (computers, desk, air conditioner, and so on), and let you focus on the show's audio.

Why Is There That Shot at the End of My Tape with the Boom Mic in It?

If you've ever asked this question (and it's okay if you have), here's the answer: At the end of shooting at each location, a good audio engineer will record room tone or natural sound. This sound is meant to be used in your Timeline to fill in any gaps.

Why? Well, there's a big difference between computer silence (the absence of any audio in the Timeline) and "true" silence. All locations on this planet have some sort of noise—whether it's the whir of machinery, the pumping of ventilation, or the chirping of birds in the background. Use the room tone between sound bites. Better yet, lay a continuous bed of it below all of your bites from a particular location. This goes a long way to smooth out the rough spots.

Narrow Your Focus

Trying to "troubleshoot" your mix? Most editors will intently listen to their video, as if intensity alone could move the edit from a "fine" cut to a "final" cut. Intent focus is a good thing, but make things a little easier by narrowing your focus. Problems will stand out in your audio track when you listen to the elements separately. Use these tips:

● Turn off your audio monitors to listen to tracks (or pairs) individually.

● If you've added audio edits to your music, do things transition smoothly, or are you trying to hide your music edits?

● Are there any loud breaths, gasps, or "guttural" sounds in your narration or sound bites? Throat clearings and coughs can be easily cleaned up.

Photo Credit Hemera Photo Objects

Little Upcuts

No matter how good of an audio editor you are, the more edits in your vocal tracks, the more likely you are to have small pops in your track. We usually add several four- or six-frame audio dissolves to all audio edits on a narration track. These short dissolves go a long way to smooth things out in your vocal track.

After adding the dissolves, be sure to listen to your mix. You want to make sure that when you add that dissolve you're not picking up extra audio clips (random words and double breaths) from the media in the clip's handles.

Pan Left	^,
Pan Center	**^.**
Pan Right	^/
Gain -3dB	^[
Gain -1dB	^-
Gain +1dB	^=
Gain +3dB	^]

Sometimes a Zero Is Good

Depending on how you capture audio, this one may really cause you problems. Be VERY careful when mixing your show for final output. You'll want to pan your narration tracks to center (or "zero them") so the voice comes out evenly from both speakers. This is true whether your audio is from a split track source (with camera and boom mic) or a single mono file imported from a CD. Follow these steps:

❶ Use the Select Track Forward tool to highlight an entire track of studio.

❷ Press Ctrl + period (.) to pan the track's center.

Pan Left	^,
Pan Center	**^.**
Pan Right	^/
Gain -3dB	^[
Gain -1dB	^-
Gain +1dB	^=
Gain +3dB	^]

Using Both Mics

Oftentimes a tape will have sound on both channels. However, it's likely that two different microphones recorded the sound. Using a camera mic and combining it with a lavaliere or boom mic often accomplishes this.

You'll want to control which mic is used. Sometimes it'll be both, sometimes only one. Be sure to adjust the levels of the two mics until things sound right. Most importantly, pan both of these mics to the center so your speakers reproduce the sound evenly.

The Road Test

One of the final steps in mixing an audio CD is the road test. Audio engineers and producers will often burn a CD, pop it in a car, and drive around town. Why? Well, it's to see how the mix sounds in a "real-world" setting.

What does this mean for you? Well, you should really try out your mix in its intended viewing area. A video meant for playback in a sports stadium will have a different mix than one going to an in-store kiosk.

Photo Credit Hemera Photo Objects

An LCD TV

One of the final techniques used to check our videos is playback on an "LCD" TV. We don't mean a fancy flat-screen set. Rather, we mean the "Least Common Denominator" television set. We keep a $150 TV/VCR combo unit around just for these purposes. It's a good idea to watch your show like the rest of the world. Joe and Jane Public don't have high-resolution monitors with a Blue-Gun for professional calibration. See things through your customer's eyes every once and a while.

This low-tech approach shouldn't replace a broadcast monitor but rather complement it. We keep both a calibrated high-end broadcast monitor and a cheap TV set in our edit suites. That way we can see both the highest and most likely denominators while we're editing our shows.

Offline-Online?

There's nothing worse than getting a Media Offline screen in the middle your show. Want a quick way to check your sequence for offline media? No problem. Follow these steps:

❶ Press Command + F to launch the Find dialog box.

❷ Select the correct project, and choose Used Media. Specify that you want to Replace Find Results.

❸ Click Find All.

❹ Look in the results box for any clips with a red line through them. You'll quickly discover any offline clips used by that sequence.

Fresh Opinion

Do your friends and loved ones hate watching movies or television with you? Chances are you critique and analyze things that others don't notice (or even care about). You're trained to notice flash frames, exposure problems, and jump cuts. But sometimes you get so close to the Canvas that you can't see the whole picture.

Find someone in your office who isn't working on the project. Better yet, grab someone who doesn't work in video at all. We used to grab the receptionist to look at all our videos. A fresh set of unbiased eyes will notice the most amazing things. Even watch your show while watching someone else is viewing it—you'll suddenly see where things work and don't work.

Photo Credit Hemera Photo Objects

Slow Down

Why take a chance of missing something? Proof your graphics while the video isn't playing. Pause on each graphic and carefully review it. Match it to your script, and carefully look for errors. A misspelled or missing word can be enough to send your 5,000 dubs rushing back to you with a change order. No matter who made the error, you were the last to "touch" it. Look carefully at your titles and lower-thirds.

When spell checking, read the copy on screen backward (no, not in a mirror, just from end to beginning!). You'll be less likely to scan too fast and miss a misspelling.

Change Your Viewpoint

If you're watching your videos in the same edit suite every day, you'll eventually develop "blind spots." Try moving things around a bit. Lay off a VHS, and take it to the conference room (or even home with you). Put a copy on your laptop, and watch it there. They key is to test it in different environments.

How to Use Your Mac's Built-in Spell Checker

Cruising through your show titles and bumpers one last time for spelling errors? It's nice to have a word processor around, but you can't afford $500 per edit system on "office" software?

Don't worry, OS X has a spell checker built right in; you just need to use TextEdit:

❶   Copy your text to your Clipboard.

❷   Switch to TextEdit, and paste the text into a new document.

❸   Choose Edit>Spelling>Spelling… or press Command + colon (:).

❹   Use the pop-up palette, and press the Find Next and Correct buttons to navigate through and correct your mistakes.

❺   When finished, select the Select All command (Command + A), and copy the text to the Clipboard (Command + C).

❻   Switch back to Final Cut Pro, and paste the new text back into your graphic.

Verify Lower Thirds and Titles

To ensure against misspelled lower-thirds and titles, get a document directly from your client with all the correct spellings or names, ranks, and serial numbers…well, you know what we mean.

Or create one yourself, and have them review and sign off on it.

Now all you need to do is copy and paste the text back into Final Cut Pro, and you've ensured that you have the clients "approved" spellings of everything!

Client Text.txt

Don't Stop

Oftentimes you'll want to play a sequence through to get the producer or client's feedback. This is a great way to get important comments to improve the show. However, they'll probably want you to stop on each "error." This is bad for several reasons. You'll lose any sense of timing or rhythm to the edit. Additionally, it's common to stop for a change, only to discover that the "missing" shot in question happens 10 seconds later.

Instead of stopping, encourage your suite mates to watch the show all the way through. Tell them you'll mark all the "problem areas."

❶ Agree on a word such as mark to signal that a shot should be flagged for review.

❷ Position the playhead at the start of the video track, and press Play.

❸ Tap the M or ` key to add a marker on the fly.

❹ Afterward, you can move between markers rapidly. Press Shift + the up or down arrows to jump between markers.

Go Low…(In Your Timeline)

Before you finish your show, try to clean the Timeline up. Get your show back down to as few of tracks as possible. Editors have a tendency to build their shows upward. Unfortunately, a "tall" show is often harder to move though because of all the scrolling. This compounds itself making it more difficult for future revisions. If you want to drag a track straight down, simply hold down the Command key when dragging.

Window Burns

You've sent your client a dub and are waiting for feedback. Eventually you get a call that goes something like this:

Client: Just got that dub and its great.... I've just got a couple of changes.

Editor: Okay, no problem.

Client: That one shot with the guy in the blue shirt...it needs to come out.

Editor: You mean just after Jane's sound bite?

Client: No, it's after the shot with the kids in it.

Repeat the previous conversation until both sides think significantly less of the other.

Want an easier way to get client feedback on a show? Make a window burn. Put the timecode across the bottom of the screen so you and your client can look at the actual timecode and reference something far more accurate than a VHS counter.

To set a sequence timecode, follow these steps:

❶   Create a new sequence with the same settings as the sequence you want to output. This will be your output sequence.

❷   Drop your edited sequence into the output sequence.

❸   Apply the Timecode Print filter to your media clip (Video Filters > Video > Timecode Print).

❹   Control + click your video track, and choose Open in Viewer.

❺   Change the mode to Reader, and it'll pick up on your sequence time.

❻   Adjust size and position so it's easier for your client to view (be sure to keep safe title area in mind).

ON THE SPOT

A Place for Everything
Media Management and Backup

One of the biggest calls for help we hear is from editors who have "misplaced" their media, render files, or entire projects. This chapter helps you plan ahead so that doesn't happen—and, if it does, where to look for them.

It's also inevitable that your client will call to make changes to last year's project, just as you empty your trash, deleting his files from your hard drive. Well, if you follow some of our backup strategies and tips, you'll have the project back online in no time (of course, billing out big bucks for those changes). All it takes is a bit of advanced planning, a CD or DVD burner, and a few good tips.

A Simple Beginning

No matter what format you shoot on or capture from, you can digitize to a lower resolution. If you have gobs of footage or want more real-time layers, consider capturing to an OfflineRT format from the beginning. Several third-party cards have their own offline formats. These low-resolution formats are a tremendous space saver. When you're done, see the tip "Back from the Trip." Remember, DV is low resolution for HD and SD.

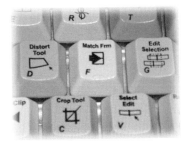

Where Did I Come From? Part One

You may want to quickly find a clip that's been edited into your Timeline. Simply park over a clip, and make sure its track is selected. Press F to match frame to the source clip. The original source should load into the Viewer with In and Out marks preserved.

Where Did I Come From? Part 2

Have a clip in your Timeline but want to find the original clip? This sounds easy—just search your Browser. But what if you have several hundred clips organized into multiple bins? Don't worry—put the computer to work. Press Shift + F to locate the clip in the Browser.

Note: This tip only works with sequences that were edited in Final Cut Pro 4.

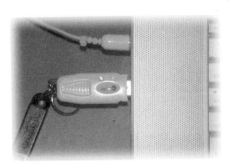

Safety Is in Your Hands (Using Portable Drives)

A project file is a very valuable thing. Consider investing in a USB thumb drive. Virtually all work under OS X and provide an excellent way to back up project files and graphics during an edit session.

"Golden Parachute" (How to Make a Perfect Backup)

We're often asked about our backup strategies. What do we save, what do we toss, where do we store things on our drives? Here's one methodology that works for us: We create two folders for each project: a "clips folder" on one of our media drives and a "golden parachute folder" on our apps drive. In the clips folder we include all captured media that we have access to that comes from the original videotape (with timecode), target all render files, and our Autosave Vault.

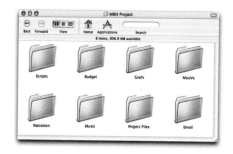

The golden folder contains everything else: our project files, graphics, still photos, music, narration, PSDs, script, budget, correspondence, and any QuickTime flies that were created in other apps. We back this folder up every time we work on this project. It has all of the elements we'd need to re-create the show minus the footage we can recapture. (Usually this all fits on a single CD-R disk, but occasionally if we have a lot of animations, we use a DVD-R.)

When the project is done, we save the archive (this folder) with the source tapes. In a year, if our client comes back to make a change, we now have everything at our fingertips, including the script and budget. (How may times have you asked your graphic artist for a file six months later only to hear, "Uh…it's somewhere…maybe on the backup server"? You'll never see that file again!) This works great.

Now when it's time to clean house, you can simply throw away your project media folder. We tend to keep golden folders on our drive as long as possible.

A Safer Vault

Your Autosave Vault backs up files to your main drive by default. In our experience, the main drive is more likely to experience corruption or damage because heavy use, viruses, and so on. A better idea is to set the Autosave Vault to archive to a different drive. This way you have extra protection if a drive or machine goes down. (A good rule of thumb is never save your project and your Autosave Vault to the same drive.)

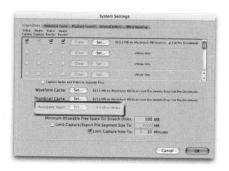

Easy Access

Moving assets into your project? Instead of dragging to the desktop (an organizational no-no), set up a shortcut to the project's golden folder. You can drag the folder icon to one of two places for easy access:

❶ Place the folder in your Dock. You can add folders on the right side of a horizontal Dock or on the bottom of a vertical Dock.

❷ You can place a shortcut to the folder in your Finder window toolbar. Just drag the folder into the striped area.

When you're done, you can easily drag these items out. Don't worry—you're not deleting them, you're just clearing the shortcut.

A Use for Old Machines and Software

I know several people who have laptops, iMacs, and blue and white G3s that won't work with Final Cut Pro 4. So what? Don't pitch them or send them off to your mother-in-law. Put them to work doing a job they can handle.

Load an old copy of Final Cut Pro 3 on that "retired" system. Old machines can be used for basic tasks such as:

● **Logging station:** Use the machine to log tape. This is especially easy for a laptop system and allows your powerful tower to be working on more demanding jobs.

● **Capture station:** If capturing from DV , most older machines can handle this task. Simply capture to external drives and save your bins. Old projects can be "promoted" to Final Cut Pro 4 projects (but you can't go the other way).

● **Cutting station:** String together shots, build basic demo reels, and cut news stories. We're all for faster machines, but certain tasks can be handled by a "lesser" computer.

● **Digital jukebox:** Use iTunes, and load your production music library. iTunes can store the files as 40kHz AIFF files (the native format for Final Cut Pro).

Stock Project

Working on an episodic television or a quarterly corporate magazine? Create a standard starting point. A master project allows you to use a template that contains all your transitions, graphics, music, lower-thirds, and so on. Follow these steps:

Video Max Show Starter

1. Take a successfully completed project, and save a copy using Save As.

2. Organize your bins for graphics, sound effects, titles, music, and so on.

3. Create subsequences for the opening, bumpers, and closing segments.

4. Close and save the project file.

5. At the Finder level, locate the project file. Highlight the project file, and press Command + I to call up the file's information. Lock the project file.

6. In the future, just launch the project. You'll have to do a Save As to save the project.

This is a great way to "fast-start" a project. All of the stock elements you need are quickly at hand. You'll save valuable time because you won't need to search and import your common files. (By the way, this tip works for daily, weekly, monthly, quarterly, and annual shows. But if you only cut once a decade, you shouldn't hold your breath.)

In-Progress Archives

What many folks don't realize is that the SuperDrives can write to a RW disc. The write speed is generally half of what it is for regular R discs, but what do you care if you're burning overnight? It's a good idea to create a project archive that contains all of your non-timecode files. You can burn to CD-RW to back up smaller projects or to DVD-RW to back up larger projects. If you find yourself archiving to disc often, be sure to check out Roxio's Toast Titanium for its streamlined approach to disc burning.

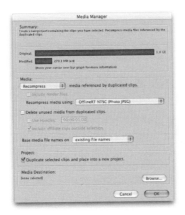

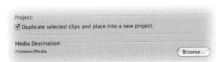

On the Road Again

Once upon a time, we dreamed of a day when we could actually get sunshine in our edit suites. Thoughts of a window and some fresh air seemed nice, but so far away. These days, we routinely get out of a dark edit suite and see the light of day (at such luxurious locations as Starbucks or Caribou Coffee).

How you ask? Offline RT. Many people write this technology off as not important. "Why work at two different resolutions? It just means more work." But this isn't the case. Offline RT is 1/8th the size of DV-25 and less than 1/40th the size of SD. On a 60GB laptop you can easily get more than 30 hours of media and still have room for most of your applications.

❶ Capture at your preferred high-quality format (DV-25, DVCPro 50, 8 bit, 10 bit, HD, and so on).

❷ With your laptop powered down, plug-in a FireWire cable between your laptop and desktop.

❸ Power up the laptop while holding down the T key. This will place the laptop in Target Disk mode. You'll see a huge bouncing FireWire icon as your desktop. Meanwhile, the laptop will appear as an icon on the primary machine's desktop. Your laptop now acts like an external hard drive that you can read and write, too. (It's a really good idea to have your laptop plugged into an electrical outlet; go ahead, do it now—we'll wait).

❹ Select all the shots and sequences in the Browser you want to move to your target disk.

❺ Contextual click, and choose Media Manager. A dialog box will appear giving you several options. There are several choices to make, but they're simple decisions.

❻ From the Media area, choose to "Recompress media referenced by duplicated clips." Choose Offline RT NTSC or Offline RT PAL depending upon your footage format.

❼ Because you intend to reference the high-resolution footage, don't delete any unused media.

⑧　Likewise, you should base media file names on existing file names.

⑨　Under the Project area, check the box to "Duplicate the selected clips and place into a new project."

⑩　Under the Media Destination area, specify a volume for the media to transcode to.

⑪　Click OK.

The speed of this process is based upon the processing speed of your computer. On a slower machine it can be timely, but the results are worth it. You'll get more layers of RT effects and zippier response from your machine. Edit away, see the world, drink lots of espresso...when you get back, it's a simple process to reconnect to the high-resolution footage.

Need to Free Up Space?

Remember, if you delete a clip from your Browser, it doesn't remove the file from your hard drive and therefore doesn't save you any space. To free up your drive, you need to delete the original media from your drives. You can do this from the Finder level or by contextual-clicking an item or items in the Browser. (See the "What's Left?" tip.) Render files can save you some space but not as much as you think. Most render files are one second (transitions) to five seconds long (a title or a filtered clip). Your big space hog is usually that one-hour tape capture where you used only 15 seconds of footage—12GB of space used for 50KB of material! Either rebatch, capture, or media manage away unused material.

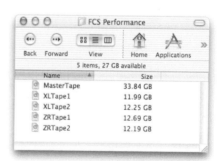

When deleting clips from the Finder, be careful. If you've used them in another project, you may end up with the dreaded "The following files are offline" message.

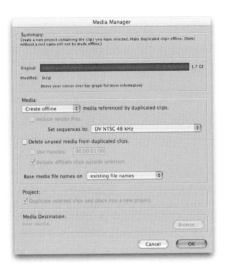

Back from the Trip: The Beginning

You've completed your project in OfflineRT and are ready to go "high-rez." The process is the same if you need to redigitize or relink to high-resolution media:

❶ Duplicate your project file. Select all the sequences and any additional clips in the Browser you want to move to your high-resolution project.

❷ Contextual click, and choose Media Manager. A dialog box will appear giving you several options.

❸ From the Media area, choose to "Create offline media referenced by duplicated clips." Set the sequence settings to match the resolution of the original media or the resolution you intend to finish in.

❹ Previous versions would frequently get confused if you deleted media from duplicated clips. Final Cut Pro 4 dramatically improves upon this. However, if the media has been previously captured, you should leave this box unchecked.

❺ Save the file to a new destination.

❻ Close the current project and the newly created project. All of the clips will come up as offline (signified by a red line slashed through the clip in the bin).

What's Left?

Need to determine what footage hasn't been used? Highlight one or more sequences, and press Command + F. Ask Final Cut Pro to show you unused media. All of the clips will be shown in the project, which can be useful when hunting for B-Roll. This way you can find shots that haven't yet been cut into your show.

Back from the Trip: Reconnecting Existing Footage

To reconnect existing footage, follow these steps:

❶ Highlight your sequence file, and contextual-click. Choose Reconnect Media, and specify to connect Offline Media.

❷ Final Cut Pro will attempt to relink the media files for you. Be careful, however, because it may default to your low-resolution footage first. Scroll left in Column view, and check which folder you're in. You may need to manually locate the high-resolution bin.

❸ Highlight the clip, and be sure that the "Reconnect All Files in Relative Path" box is checked.

❹ Continue reconnecting until the project is online. You'll need to rerender all effects.

Back from the Trip: Capturing at a Higher Resolution

To capture at a higher resolution, follow these steps:

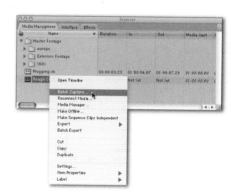

❶ Highlight your sequence file, and contextual-click. Choose Batch Capture.

❷ Capture your media using standard workflow.

❸ Highlight any graphic and sound files, and choose to reconnect media.

❹ You'll need to rerender all effects.

"Master Backup Project"

This tip is useful if you're upgrading from Final Cut Pro 3 to 4, moving from system to system, or deleting your Final Cut Pro 4 user preferences. A lot of folks don't realize you can drag a favorite/custom filter, motion, or transition directly into your Browser. Create a project and label it as **Master Backup**. Now drag your Favorites folder out from your Effects tab, and drop it into your project tab of your Browser. Also, if you've created any titles or lower-thirds that you want to save for future use, open their projects and drag them across into your Master Backup project. Save this project. You now have a backup of all your favorites to restore on your machine, to another user account, or to transfer to another edit system.

.mac Has Got Your Back

Apple offers an excellent service for online storage, tools, and utilities. One of those utilities is Backup, which is designed to synchronize some of your key system settings. Any file can be added to Backup and be told to archive to your iDisk (the Internet storage that comes with a .mac account). Be sure to add your active project file to the backup list and tell it to archive every night. This is an excellent way to preserve a clean copy of the project file.

Backup

Out of Space?

Running out of disk space fast? Well, you can delete media without throwing away logging information. Remember, with all of the clip information, you can always recapture material that has timecode.

1 Press Command + F to launch the Find dialog box.

2 Select Unused media from the dialog box, and click Find All.

3 In the Results window, select all the clips.

4 Contextual-click, and select Make Offline.

5 Choose either "Delete Them from the Disk" option if you're confident.

Alternatively, you can choose "Move Them to the Trash" if you want a "trial" delete. Check your sequence to make sure no media went offline unintentionally. The easiest way to do this is to contextual-click the sequence icon, and select Relink Media. If the Offline box is grayed out, there are no clips offline. Erase whenever you want.

The key advantage of this method is that you're not throwing away logging information. If you discover you need a clip in the future, you can easily recapture the clip.

We Do It Every Night

It's ESSENTIAL to make a backup copy of your project at the end of an edit session. Creating a thumb drive, burning removable disc, even emailing yourself the file is a great way to make a copy of your work. When you least expect it, things will go wrong. As long as you have a copy of the project file and your source tapes (with timecode), restoring a project is a fast process. BACKUP NOW...or regret it later.

If you have a .mac account, set it up to automatically back up your active project's folder.

ON THE SPOT

Didn't Know It Could
Secrets of the Power Users

The goal of this chapter is to show you a bunch of cool tricks that we hope will not only impress your clients but you, as well.

Final Cut Pro is an incredibly robust editing tool. In the right hands, with the right creativity, and with a bit of knowledge, you should be able to re-create anything you see in movies or on television.

The key is knowing what the application can do, seeing an effect you like, and then trying to "reverse engineer" how it was done. We've provided some shortcuts to this reverse-engineering process. Take our ideas, and run with them; you'll be amazed at what a little creative manipulation can achieve. By the end of the chapter, you should be saying, "Wow, I didn't know it could do that!" But your clients should just be saying, "Wow."

Photo credit James Ball

Wiggle It!

Nearly everywhere you see titles and graphics shaking and wiggling. Here's how to do it in Final Cut Pro without setting a single keyframe. All you need is some shaky video and a title or graphic created in an outside graphics program. Then follow these steps:

1 Create a really tall sequence. This is done by first creating a normal-sized sequence, opening it in the Timeline, hitting Command + 0, changing its Aspect Ratio to Custom, and setting its height to around 1,000. Name the sequence something like **Tall Nest**.

2 Edit the shaky video into V1, and move it to the bottom of the tall frame.

3 Superimpose the graphic into V2 above the shaky video, and move it to the top of the tall frame.

4 Create a new normal-sized sequence, edit Tall Nest into this new sequence, and move the playhead to the first frame. In the Canvas window, Tall Nest should appear oversized but centered on the screen.

5 Apply Video Filters > Video > Image Stabilizer to the Tall Nest, and set your Scan Area on a high-contrast, unobscured spot of the shaky video. Adjust the Scan Range according to how shaky your video is. (Remember: To load a nest into the Viewer to access its Filter parameters, Option + double-click it in the Timeline.)

6 Move Tall Nest down so that only its top half with the graphic is visible, and render. Because the graphic is nested with the shaky video, it'll appear to wiggle as the Image Stabilizer tracks the motion in the video.

Christopher Phrommayon, Future Media Concepts

What You Want

The auto-select buttons help let you work with only on the tracks you want. Say you want to delete video from tracks 1, 2, and 5 but leave tracks 3 and 4 alone. Simply auto-select tracks 1, 2, and 5, mark and In and an Out point in the Timeline, and delete. They're gone, and tracks 3 and 4 are untouched. Ripple delete works, too...but be careful, you may throw your Timeline out of sync.

Steal More (Attributes)

We stumbled across this trick while working on videos for a conference. In building the opening video, we had an effects-intensive piece cut to music. The client decided to edit a closing video with footage from the event. They wanted a "similar" look to both videos.

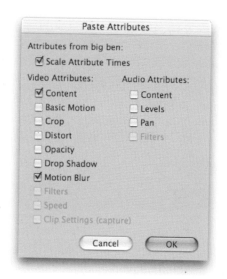

We simply duplicated the sequence and quickly re-edited the video. Here's how:

❶   Pick the replacement shot. Mark an In Point where you'd like the shot to begin.

❷   Copy the shot by pressing Command + C.

❸   Highlight the destination in your Timeline with the select tool.

❹   Contextual-click, and choose Paste Attributes. Select Content for the Video (audio if wanted).

❺   The new shot replaces the old. It's the same duration and has all of the same effects applied.

This is a huge timesaver when building bumpers, lower-thirds, promos, or any other type of edit where there's repetition.

Subclip without a Mouse

It's often helpful to subclip a larger clip into more manageable chunks. Oftentimes you can subclip a long interview into shorter responses or a long B-Roll clip into specific shots. In all cases, this is nondestructive editing, thus leaving the larger original clip untouched. Follow these steps:

❶   While viewing a clip in the Browser, you can use J-K-L to navigate.

❷   Mark In and Out points using the I and O keys.

❸   When you have the desired region, press Command + U to create a subclip.

❹   The clip is automatically selected in the Browser. Name it, and then press Enter.

❺   Press Command + 1 to return to the Viewer, or press Command + 2 to return to the Canvas.

Photo credit James Ball

Fill the Screen

Giving a demo or just want to make an area bigger to show the client what you're working on? Under OS X you have a Zoom feature that's part of Universal Access. Designed to help those visually impaired, it's quite useful for focusing on small elements or taking the Canvas monitor full-screen:

1 Press Command + Option + 8 to enable the feature or go to the Universal Access System Preferences pane. Be patient because it takes a few seconds to launch.

2 Press Command + Option + + (the plus sign) to zoom in.

3 Press Command + Option + - (the minus sign) to zoom out.

4 Press Command + Option + 8 to disable the feature when you're done.

Warp of Distortion

The Distort parameters in the Motion tab are great for corner pinning, but if you go back to junior-high art class and remember how perspective and vanishing points work, you can use Distort parameters to simulate 3D space. Follow these steps:

1 First, crop any video blanking that may appear on the edges of your video images.

2 Next, you need to understand how the Distort parameters' coordinate system works. The center of the object is at (0, 0), right is positive on the X axis, and down is positive on the Y axis. (Note: The Y axis is the exact opposite of the Cartesian coordinate system you learned in geometry class.)

3 Because each of the corners of a video object can be moved and keyframed, you can position and animate them to create a sense of perspective and the illusion of 3D space. If you prefer to drag, hold down the Command key. This way the opposite corner will move an equal amount to the corner you're dragging.

4 Whenever distorting DV material in this way, you may notice some artifacts. If so, increasing the Edge Feather setting in the Crop parameter and applying a slight Gaussian Blur may help.

5 Activating the drop shadow may emphasize the 3D look.

Photo credit James Ball

Christopher Phrommayon, Future Media Concepts

Why You Need Batch Capture

Have you ever needed to go on a road trip across state lines or to a location out of town? Some people forget the first rule of video (plan!), and just jump in the car and try to go instantly. This option is prone to many issues.

Several editors we meet don't harness the power of the Batch Capture feature. They rely on the inefficient Capture Clip or, worse, the potentially dangerous Capture Now. So what's the big deal? The video goes into the computer, right?

Getting into capture mode takes time. You'll see increased stability and efficiency if you do all of your capturing at once. Plus, performing a batch capture lets you put the computer to work while you change gears. Let the computer spend 30 minutes capturing on its own, and you can work on picking music, switch to a second machine and work on graphics in LiveType or Photoshop, or even just return voice and email.

Follow these steps:

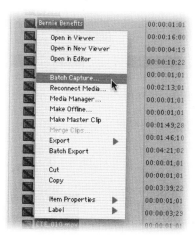

❶　Define which bin is your logging bin. This is where clips will be stored. It's a good idea to have a separate bin per source tape. This makes it easier to batch capture and archive.

❷　Review and log your footage. Mark In and Out points like always. When a clip is defined, click the Log Clip button or press F2.

❸　Before a batch capture, save your project. Bringing video in is one of the most demanding tasks on the application. You're most likely to crash during capture.

❹　When ready, click Batch Capture or press Control + C. You can only batch capture if your camera or deck supports device control. Most FireWire devices and professional video decks are supported. You may need to get a special deck control cable and USB to serial adapter to use older professional decks.

❺　The best part of the Batch Capture feature is that it's an automated process. You can leave your system unattended while it captures the logged clips. So your system will not hiccup, you'll need to change a few preferences. Under the General Settings tab, be sure to uncheck the "Abort capture on dropped frames" and "Abort capture on timecode break" boxes.

A More Useful Subclip

When you create a subclip, it can't access the original media. This may cause problems if you need to trim or add a transition. It's a good idea to remove subclip limits. This command can be done to a group of subclips.

❶ Select the subclip(s) in your Browser window.

❷ Choose Modify> Remove Subclip Limits.

Slowly Trim the Dynamic Trim

But what if you want to roll the edit point more slowly? This tip will come in handy when trying to trim around syllables:

❶ Select the edit point with the roll edit tool or select tool, and double-click.

❷ Hold down the K key and use J or L to roll the edit point left or right at quarter speed.

❸ When you find the edit point, release the K key first to establish the new edit point.

Stealing Render Files

Sometimes if we've created a clip with a complex effect (that took a while to render), we actually go into our Render Files folder and pull out that file (render files are simply QuickTime movies and work like self-contained clips). This can then be edited on the video track above the layered/effected shot. This way the effect can't be "unrendered" by visibility changes or adding titles.

Now, how do you know which render file is which? Well, your render files are sorted by project (you may also find it useful to sort by date modified). And full resolution render files have "FIN" in their title. Here's the trick: Open the Render folder in Column view. Drill down to the project on which you're working. You can preview any of the clips directly in the Finder (while in Column view) by selecting them and clicking the Play button.

Instant Money

Here's an example of how Final Cut Pro is a license to make money. Your client comes to you with 100 digital pictures that need to be turned into a slide show set to music. In the old days, this would be an arduous and boring tasks. No more.

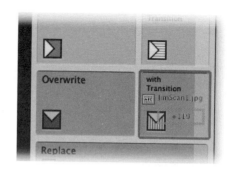

First, do the math...no, not how much profit you are going to make but how long the slide show needs to be. A good length to view each slide is about five seconds. So you need a cut of music about 8 1/3 minutes long. (Hint: Soundtrack is great for this.) Follow these steps:

❶ Set your Still/Freeze duration to five seconds. You can access this in your user preferences (Option + Q).

❷ Take the folder filled with the still images and sort them, assigning each a number 001, 002, 003, and so on (or sort them later in the Icons view in the Browser).

❸ Choose File>Import Folder, or drag the folder from the Finder into the browser.

❹ All of the stills are imported with a duration of five seconds (don't worry; you'll have almost a minute-long handle on each side for those loooong dissolves).

❺ Pick a good transition and make it your default transition. By the way, a cross-dissolve is a good transition in this case.

❻ Highlight and drag all the clips from the Browser into the Canvas of your desired sequence, and drop it on "overwrite with transition."

Hmm, 8 1/3 minutes long. Drop on your music, and—poof!—it's done. Four hours of work done in 15 minutes. Bill your clients a flat fee for these types of projects. They'll be happy because they just saved 50 percent over the four-hour bid from the other post house. You, on the other hand, did the work in 1/8th of that time, so what should you do with that extra hour and 45 minutes? Well, you could laugh all the way to the bank.

Save the Layout

All Timeline layouts can be saved so you can quickly call them up. Next to the Toggle Timeline Track Height bars is a submenu. Simply arrange the Timeline how you want, and turn on the desired view options. Then save it.

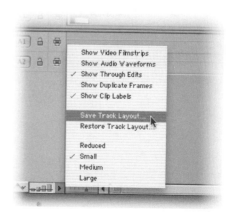

Instant Money with Style

Let's say you want to notch that slide show up a bit. Make it move a little. The magic phrase here is slow moves...seasick clients aren't happy clients. Follow these steps:

1 Select a clip, and apply scale keyframes; for example, start at 110 percent and end at 100 percent.

2 Define this as a favorite motion path by pressing Control + F.

3 Repeat the process on another clip, and scale from 100 percent to 110 percent.

4 Define this as a favorite motion path as well.

5 You can define up to nine favorite motion paths. In fact, you can even map these as buttons to any button bar.

6 Now highlight several clips; click the path you want. Repeat. Repeat. Repeat. Done!

Time Remapping (Through Editing!)

Time is an illusion in video: You control how and what you see. To show the effect of passing time, the following are a couple of editing tricks:

- **Distance:** As a subject moves away from you over a period of time, you get the illusion. To visually speed the process, a series of straight cuts shows the movement. (Think of someone walking–but you only see them every 20 feet or so as they walk away).

- **Light:** Movement of light on a set gives the illusion of time. On set remember that short passing shot of light moving slowing across a tabletop gives the feeling that time is passing just as if you were watching the afternoon passing.

- **Color:** Desaturation of color over time gives the illusion of passing time, also. We've seen this in Hollywood for so long we expect that when the image passes from color to black and white (or vice versa), time has passed between the different looks.

Gary Adcock, Studio 37, Founder and President of the Chicago FCP User Group

Defocusing DV Background Footage

Note that most of the consumer/prosumer DV cameras have way too much depth of field. This is because of the small size of the CCD chips. In pro cameras the size of the chip is nearly 2x as large. This is great if all your shooting is exteriors, but if you're shooting an interview close-up it may mean that too much of your background will be in focus. A sharp focus background is disconcerting to the average viewer.

The solution is to follow these steps:

❶ Edit your clip first—if you're doing a reverse (showing both the interviewer and subject), edit your entire sequence first.

❷ Clone the clip to the track above. Select the clip, and then drag while holding down Option + Shift to create a clone directly above.

❸ Create a mask by selecting Effects> Video Filters > Matte > Garbage Matte / Image Shape / Image Mask (choose one type of mask, not all three), and center the area over the main focus point on the top image.

❹ Use Video Filters > Matte > Mask Feather to soften the edges.

❺ On the original layer of the project, add a blur—not too much to start, maybe five to ten pixels. This will give your video a "filmic" short-focus look.

Gary Adcock, Studio 37, Founder and President of the Chicago FCP User Group

Photo credit Time Image (http://www.timeimage.com)

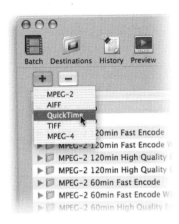

LiveType Backgrounds in Real-Time Using Compressor Droplets

LiveType renders everything in the Animation codec. This is advantageous for two reasons. First, it's uncompressed—meaning you can use the resulting animation, type, and so on in any sequence type (DV, SD, HD) or, for that matter, other nonlinear editing systems. Second, the Animation codec supports an alpha channel—a channel that defines what parts of the image are transparent. Note that Apple's DV codec doesn't support an alpha channel.

Bearing this in mind, when you bring any LiveType movie into Final Cut Pro, you'll always get a render warning. Why? Because LiveType is using a different codec than your sequence—the vast majority of Final Cut Pro users are working in DV. Anytime you mix codecs, Final Cut Pro has to recompress, hence the red render bars.

But what if you only want to export a background from LiveType to use in Final Cut Pro? You can use Compressor to recompress the LiveType movies to make them the DV codec (or any other real-time codec your system supports). When they're put into Final Cut Pro, they'll be real-time items.

Follow these steps:

❶ Open Compressor.

❷ Hit the plus button to create a new preset. Choose QuickTime.

❸ Go to the bottom of the list (because it's now named Untitled QuickTime). Select it, and click the Encoder tab.

❹ Disable Audio, and then click Video Settings.

❺ From the pop-up menu, choose DV/DVCPRO-NTSC, and make sure the Motion setting is 29.97 frames per second. Set the Quality to Best. Click OK.

❻ Go to the Geometry tab, and change the Output size to 100 percent of source.

❼ Change the name from Untitled QuickTime to Convert to DV by double-clicking the name.

❽ Make this a droplet by clicking the little down arrow with a dot in the upper-right corner.

⑨   Have the Droplet Destination option be Source (same as where the original movie was), and put the droplet wherever you'd like it to live.

⑩   Now drag and drop LiveType Animation codec movies, and they'll be converted to DV codec movies. We've had to have Compressor already running in the background for this to automatically work. When used in Final Cut Pro, there will be no red render bar.

> Note: If there's a red render bar in Final Cut Pro, check your LiveType project settings and make sure you're set to DV 720x480.

Jeff I. Greenberg. Principal Instructor, Future Media Concepts

Get to the Good Stuff (Easy Access to Your Settings)

We used to have an old leather chair that fit us very well...we like our editing system to feel the same way. Saving your preferences is a good thing, but taking them with you from system to system is even better.

To always have your user settings at hand, make your Final Cut Pro User Data a favorite. You can quickly find your settings by searching for Final Cut Pro User Data at the Finder level. Highlight the folder, and press Command + T to make something a favorite item. Now you can quickly find your settings, and move them with a thumb drive to your next edit job.

Power Log

Did you realize you can log faster than real-time? Try these three tips to get your footage in fast:

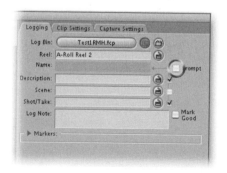

●   Simply tap the L button multiple times to play the tape faster. With practice you can ramp your playback speed up and still understand the dialogue. All of your logging controls still work.

●   Better yet, log while viewing. Tap I to mark an In point, and then press F2 to simultaneously add the outpoint and log the clip.

●   Uncheck the prompt box in the logging window. After you name the first clip, all subsequent clips will be progressively numbered or lettered.

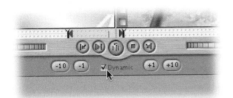

Trim the Dynamic Trim

Final Cut Pro 4 allows you to roll a trim point left or right from the keyboard. Double-click an edit point, and you switch to trim mode. You can now use J and L to roll the editing point dynamically:

❶ Enter trim mode by double-clicking between two clips with either the selection tool (A) or the roll edit tool (R).

❷ Be sure to click Enable Dynamic trimming button at the bottom of the trim window.

❸ Trim left by pressing J or right by pressing L. You can hear the audio in real-time.

❹ Press K to stop trimming.

Bar None? No, Bar All.

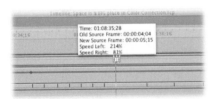

You've built a great button bar and have all the tools you need within one mouse click. Now idiot-proof it, and save that bar. Contextual-click the bar, and choose Save Main Button Bars. All of your button bars are stored in one setting in your User Preferences folder.

Time Remap in the Timeline

Final Cut Pro 4 has added some great time adjustment tools, replicating the similarly functioning TimeBender plug-in from Joe's Filters. It's also capable of allowing variable time adjustment without cutting or "blading" the track when changing speed. The advantage is that the clip length is no longer modified when using a variable adjustment.

The Time Remap Tool is behind the Slip and Slide tools accessed by typing SSS on your keyboard. The icon appears as a small stopwatch, and it allows you to dynamically adjust your frame rate from the Timeline. To view the keyframe adjustment, make sure you select User Preferences | Timeline Options to check the "Speed Indicators" box and then turn on Clip Keyframes (Option + T or click the railroad tracks at the bottom left of the Timeline window).

Gary Adcock, Studio 37, Founder and President of the Chicago FCP User Group

Master of Time

Need to change your playback speed? Easy, right? Just press Command + J. But what if you want the video to ramp up or slow down gradually? That's what time remapping is for. You'll need some practice with the tool to get the hang of it, but don't try to control it in the Timeline with the Time Remap feature. It's much easier to see your keyframes in the Viewer.

Follow these general guidelines:

- Keyframes indicate original video frames. If you add a keyframe at the 3:00 mark, then pull it forward to 1:15, the video will play back at double speed until that keyframe and then slow down afterward.

- Keyframes closer together create steeper slopes, which mean faster playback.

- Keyframes further apart create gradual slopes, which mean slower speeds.

- Make sure Frame Blending is turned on.

- Use the Smooth Point Tool (ppp) to improve the movement between keyframes. Bezier curves are your friend.

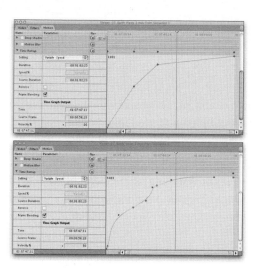

ON THE SPOT

CHAPTER 15

Out of the Box
Exporting and Publishing Your Program

Good editors think outside the box, and great editors don't even know there's a box. (The best editors are kept in a box and only let out to edit!) We hope this book has already allowed you to exceed the limitations of your box. With that said, this chapter focuses on mastering and delivering your magnum opus.

The days of delivering just a video master are long gone. Clients now expect you to multipurpose their shows. In addition to a tape version, you're often asked for a DVD master, a CD master, multiple Web versions, a streaming audio file, and even frame grabs.

This means you must once again wear many hats beyond just being an editor. That's okay because this chapter will make a hat rack out of you.

Full Screen Preview

Want to play back your sequence full screen on your computer monitor? People graduating from iMovie will likely miss its View Clips in Full-Screen mode. Final Cut Pro doesn't have the same feature (why?). QuickTime Pro, however, does, and you can use it for full-screen playback:

❶ Export a QuickTime movie of your sequence.

❷ Don't double-click the file. Rather, launch QuickTime Pro, and manually open the movie from the File menu.

❸ Press Shift + Command + F to present the movie. If you have more than one screen, select which screen you want it to play on.

For the best results, set your monitor's resolution to its lowest setting. This will reduce pixilation.

Watermark Your Stuff

Have an approval copy that you need to send out? Want to make sure people realize it's a draft and not made for public display? Or have a new client you want to make sure pays you? Mark the program as an Approval Copy, Private, Not for Public Showing, and so on. Follow these steps:

❶ Create a new sequence that has the same settings as your show.

❷ Drag your completed show into the Canvas window, and drop it on the Overwrite box.

❸ Go to the Viewer, and load the Text Generator. Adjust the text settings. If you need the text to be longer than its current limits, type in a new duration in the Timecode Duration field of the Viewer.

❹ Edit the title on top of your video clip. Adjust the Opacity setting to approximately 15 percent, and position it at the bottom of the screen.

Under Final Cut Pro 4, this effect can be real-time if your processor is fast enough.

Crash to VHS

Because Final Cut Pro 4 supports sending out over FireWire without rendering, it's possible to go to VHS without rendering. That being said, you'll drop frames, and it may not play back everything correctly. So balance your deadline with the client's ability to understand what "rough cut" means. Follow these steps:

1. Check your playback settings in the Timeline. You'll want to choose Unlimited RT.

2. Depending on your processor speed, select Low or Medium playback quality.

3. To free up overhead for the video effects, mix down your audio track. This is a very fast procedure compared to rendering your video effects.

4. Close the windows you don't need open, and close any other open applications, as well.

5. Make sure the signal is going out over FireWire by choosing View > External Video > All Frames (or pressing Command + F12).

6. Park your cursor at the start of the Timeline, start your deck, and press Record. After 10 seconds, press Play in the Timeline. It's a good idea to turn off the "Report dropped frames during playback" option under User Preferences.

Output from Timeline Draft or Full Quality

When outputting a sequence, use the RT pop-up menu in the Timeline to quickly determine if Final Cut Pro should render everything to full quality before output or to just play back the sequence in real-time with your lower-resolution RT settings. This is really useful if you need to make a quick approval dub for the client to take with them or if the FedEx pick-up guy is pounding on your door.

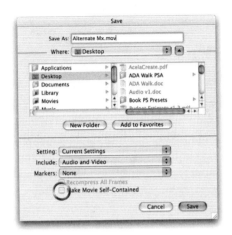

Reference Movies

Need to save some space? Reference movies allow you to work with your video clips or sequence files in other applications. Think of a reference movie as a pointer back to the original media, a lot like a link on a web page. Follow these steps:

❶ Choose File>Export QuickTime Movie.

❷ Name the file, and choose to not make the movie self-contained. This will save you disk space by referencing back to the media on your local drives. That being said, the media can't be deleted, moved, or on a different machine that's unreachable via a network.

❸ Import the file into your other video application, and start working.

Reference movies are useful when working in After Effects, Cleaner, iDVD, or other apps where you want to work with a large video file. This is a useful way to export a sequence or longer segment of clips as one file. If you want to permanently save the video clip, be sure to check the "Self-Contained" box. Just remember that an hour-long show at DV quality will need more than 12GB of space!

A Cheaper 'DVD' part 1

Need to test your DVD for computer playback? You want to see how the whole thing plays back from the optical drive (any skipping or crashes)? Tired of wasting discs? It's possible to burn your DVD content to a CD for playback on a computer. If the computer has a drive that can read both CDs and DVDs, then this trick works fine:

❶ Simply author your disc, and save the VIDEO_TS and AUDIO_TS folders.

❷ Burn these folders to a data disc using Toast or other third-party disc-burning application.

❸ In Apple's DVD Player application, choose File > Open VIDEO_TS Folder. Navigate to the TS folder on the CD, and open the file.

A Cheaper DVD, Part 2

If you're using Toast to burn your DVDs, you can harness the power of a DVD-RW. Not all players will recognize a rewriteable disc, but if yours does, a DVD-RW is a great way to save money during the testing stage.

Slates: What Needs to Be There?

Slates are useful for a lot of things. The following are what we put on ours (and why). These aren't the only things you might try, but it's a good place start:

- **Title of show:** That way the duplicator or broadcaster knows the right tape is in the machine without having to fast-forward into your show.

- **Run time:** Duplicators are really happy when they put the right length tape in their recorders, and broadcasters like to know if that spot is 30 seconds or a minute.

- **Audio mix:** Mixed, discreet tracks, stereo, mono, and multiple languages are lots of options. And don't forget to tell them what levels your tone is set to: –12db, –18db, –20db, or even 0db if you're going analog.

- **Date and version:** If you do lots of version of a show or a weekly show, adding the date helps stop confusion.

- **Production company:** They lost the box, and now they know who the production company is—oh yeah, when the network loves the show, they know who to hire!

- **Phone number:** Now they know how to get a hold of you to praise your work—or curse you if your levels are all messed up.

- **Audio:** If you're combining a slate with your countdown, you may want to add audio. Use short beeps that match the tone under your bars. There should be no audio or picture after the 2-pop on your tape.

Stomp It

Need to make clips smaller? Final Cut Pro has an excellent compression utility built in. If you intend to output to MPEG-2 or MPEG-4, Compressor is your application of choice:

❶ Mark an In and Out Point on your Timeline to define the range.

❷ Choose File > Export > Using Compressor.

❸ Specify one or more settings from the preset list. Submit the job, and let it run.

❹ If you're in a hurry, close your other open applications and let the compression tie up all your system resources.

You can also create additional presets for QuickTime encoding. All codecs (including third-party ones) that are properly installed will be available.

> Note: If you need to know more on compression, check out Compression for Great Digital Video by Ben Waggonner.

Better Stomp for MPEG-4

If the presets in Compressor don't quite fit your need, tweak them! By clicking the Presets icon, you can call up lists of all the presets that Compressor uses. All you need to do is modify an existing preset, or make your own from scratch.

The following are some options to try:

● For bit rate, the VBR options (which stands for variable bit rate) produce smaller file sizes and better quality. They take longer, however, because the processing time increases.

● Cutting the frame rate in half is a great way to save space. Something that originated in NTSC looks great at 15 frames per second for playback on a computer.

● Adjust the Audio Bit Rate setting. If you have the bandwidth (and the audio is important), increase it. A talking head, on the other hand, can be more compressed before you'll notice a big difference in quality.

Tips on Compression

The art of compressing files for the web or disc is a technology art form that stumps many people. With hundreds of options, settings, and sliders, it's no wonder. To demystify things a bit, here's a crash course on getting your file size down.

To start, have a five-minute QuickTime movie with DV NTSC compression at full size that's approximately 1GB. Then follow these steps:

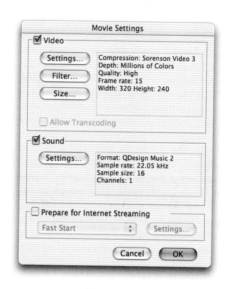

❶ Reduce the frame rate to 15 frames per second (512MB).

❷ Reduce to Half Screen 320¥240. This cuts both the height and width in half, as well as compensates for non-square pixels. If your compression application supports cropping, be sure to crop 10 percent of all sides to compensate for the space outside of Action Safe. (You're now at 128MB.)

❸ If you have the option, be sure to deinterlace the video track. Interlaced video is for playback on a television, not a computer.

❹ You may also consider reducing the sample rate and size. The same math benefits apply. Reducing an audio track from 48kHz to 22kHz saves more than 2¥ space on the audio side. You're also likely to be able to go to an 8-bit mono file if it's for playback on a typical PC. Those two options combined will shave 75 percent off the audio file size.

❺ Add audio compression to taste; IMA 4:1, QDesign, and MP3 work well depending on your source material.

❻ Save the output settings as a preset or write them down. This way you can troubleshoot client changes or just replicate the settings on the next job because the client liked the results so well.

Entire Media

Getting ready to Print to Video or Edit to Tape? Be sure to specify that you want to print the "Entire Media"; otherwise you'll only output between your In and Out points (useful if you mean to, but a pain if you didn't). In and Out marks will often affect exporting as well, so be sure to mark the area you want or clear the In and Out marks.

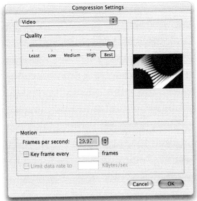

When Video Is the Wrong Answer

When exporting a video clip, you're probably often asked to set the compression method. These codecs (compressor/decompressor) are the method used to shrink file size. The following is an overview of the top choices.

Video	Video is a legacy codec and goes back to one of the earliest forms of compression available. It's ancient and results in very poor image quality.
Animation	Useful when sending a file to be processed by another application, especially if several different motion graphic artists and animators need to process the file.
None	No compression, a full-frame size. This can be useful when archiving a clip.
Sorenson 3	An update to the Sorenson codec, which can be used for CD-ROM or web delivery. It requires QuickTime 5 or newer for playback.

In all cases, try to avoid double compression. Work with as high of quality source file as possible, then compress at the very end.

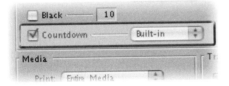

Count Down: "In 3...2...1"

Countdowns are generally not needed on your master tape. People seem enamored by countdowns, though (maybe it's the fault of Wayne's World). You generally need a countdown in the following situations; otherwise, leave it off:

1. If the piece is going on air, put a countdown on it. This includes news packages, programming, commercials, and video news releases.

2. If the piece is for playback at a live event, put a countdown on it for cueing purposes. Make it a subdued countdown (such as small, dark gray numbers over black), and keep it silent.

3. If the client specifically asks you for one.

Video CD

The Video CD format is a precursor to the DVD. You can fit approximately one hour of video on a CD-ROM using MPEG-1 compression. The quality is similar to a VHS and doesn't match that of a DVD. If you install Toast Titanium, Video CD is an option. Follow these steps:

1. Export a QuickTime movie of your sequence by choosing File | Export | QuickTime Movie (if you want to save this file for future compression, choose to make the movie self-contained).

2. Launch Toast Titanium. From the Other menu in the main window, choose Video CD.

3. Drag the QuickTime movie into the source window, and click Record.

Toast Titanium will compress the Video CD and author the disc. It will play back in several DVD players (but not all).

PTV (What's That?)

Want to go straight to tape when you choose Print to Video without having to press Record on your deck and click OK? You need to turn on Auto Record and PTV after three seconds. To access this advanced control, you need to call up your Audio/Video Settings folder:

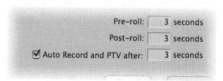

1. Choose Final Cut Pro > Audio/Video Settings.

2. Go to the Device Control Presets tab, and modify your current deck control preset that has worked for you.

3. Check the "Auto Record and PTV after: X seconds" box, and specify a time to wait. Three seconds is usually enough.

   Note: The PTV setting is a function of your camera and deck and may not be supported by all devices. This is a hardware option, not a software setting.

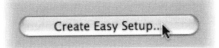

Making Presets

Hardware settings can be tricky. We can't tell you how to configure every third-party device you may want to add to your system such as a DV converter, but we can suggest a few things to make life easier:

● RTFM: Be sure to check with the manufacturer on how to configure your audio/video settings. Many devices have very specific options to get their decks or converter boxes working "seamlessly."

● When it works, save it. Be sure all device control presets and A/V devices are named and saved.

● With the correct settings active, create an easy setup. This will allow you to change settings from one menu. It isn't uncommon to have several configurations for capture and output depending on the hardware devices you have hooked to your system. These are stored inside your Custom Settings folder (<System Drive>>Library > Application Support > Final Cut Pro Support > Custom Settings). You should back this folder up anytime you add easy setups.

Audio Mixdown...Where Are You?

When outputting material to tape, an Audio Mixdown feature was a recommended precaution to ensure you didn't drop frames. In Final Cut Pro 4, however, the option has moved from its familiar place. Choose Sequence > Render Only > Mixdown (or press Command + Option + R). You can also map this as a button, and place it into the Timeline button bar.

Convert Between QuickTime and Avid

Have a bunch of animation files that were made for an Avid editing project? You may have some show graphics around that were compressed with AVR 77 or Avid 2:1. As long as you have the Avid codec installed on your system (it's free from the support page at Avid's site), you can convert. Follow these steps:

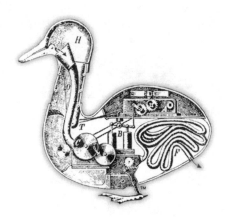

❶ Follow the steps described in the "Use Converter" tip.

❷ Add the files to Compressor's window by drag and drop. The QuickTime codec will properly decode the files.

❸ Batch process to the format you need.

This conversion can happen in the Timeline as well, but batching the files proves faster from a workflow point of view.

> Note: If you need to do a lot of conversion, be sure to check out Automatic Duck's utilities for importing and exporting between Final Cut Pro, Avid products, After Effects, and Boris RED 3GL. They're truly a timesaver if you do a lot of work between programs.

QuickTime Installers

Sending your client a QuickTime file? You may want to give them the installer on the CD-ROM. QuickTime Player is a free program and is fully cross-platform. You can download the installers from Apple's website. You can find the self-contained installers at www.apple.com/quicktime/download/standalone/. If your client has web access, you can save the address by dragging it from your Address Bar to the desktop.

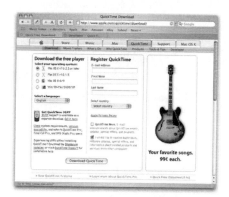

Send Your Client an MP3

Have a client with low-bandwidth? Consider sending them an MP3 of your program. We'll often do this when we want to lock in an audio mix for a piece that's music dependant or after the rough cut is complete on a documentary-style piece. Follow these steps:

❶ Choose File Export to AIFF(s).

❷ Export at a sample rate of 48kHz, a sample size of 16 bit, and the files at the Stereo Mix setting. Starting with a high-quality source file will result in better compression.

❸ Import the resulting file into iTunes. You can drag it into the library, or choose File | Import.

❹ In iTunes, you need to set your MP3 settings. Go to iTunes > Preferences, and then click the Importing tab. The MP3 Encoder and Good Quality settings work well.

❺ Highlight the track you want to convert.

❻ Choose Advanced > Convert Selection to MP3. iTunes will convert your AIFF into an MP3 file quickly.

By default, the file will be added to your library. Simply select the MP3 file in your iTunes window, and press Command + R to reveal the file. Email it to your client, and wait for feedback. Both Windows and Mac machines have the ability to play back MP3 files built into any modern operating system.

Deliver on Disc...Test on Disc

If you intend to deliver a file on CD or DVD, you need to burn the file to disc and then play it back. Why? Well, the file may be too large and exceed the data rate of your playback device. Don't assume that your client has a 52¥-rated drive. Burn to CD, and test it in on a machine that's similar to your client's. Once you have a working setting that your client is happy with, be sure to save it and use it in the future.

"I'm Working...Really!" (Using Actions)

Compressor supports actions. One of the coolest features is sending an email notification. You can set this up to ping you at your desk. For those on the move (with cell phone in hand), you can send yourself a note. Most cell phones support text messages; simply contact your phone service provider for specific instructions.

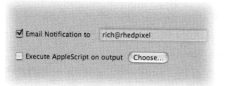

A Loop is A Loop is A Loop

Need to make a show loop for a client's tradeshow booth or front entry? Final Cut Pro makes it easy for you to make money. In the Print to Video or Edit to Tape dialog boxes, you can specify how many times a show should loop. You can also add black in between each segment. Feel free to use the bars and tone options because they'll only be added to the first pass; all of the loops will contain just the program content.

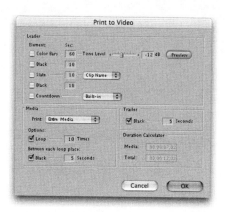

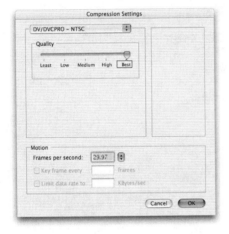

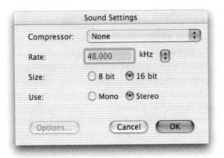

Converter

You can repurpose Compressor as a converter. Let's say you have a large collection of stock animations that are the wrong size, frame rate, and so on. This is very likely when working with stock clips that you want to cut into a DV project. Simply create a preset that matches your sequence settings.

To convert to NTSC DV, follow these steps:

❶ In Compressor, call up the Presets window by clicking the Presets icon.

❷ Add a new preset by clicking the Create a New Preset button (the plus sign).

❸ Specify QuickTime as the encoder.

❹ In the Settings area at the bottom, use the following settings for the Encoder tab:

a. Video

- DV/DVCPRO – NTSC
- Best Quality
- 29.97 frames per second
- Don't limit the data rate

b. Audio

- Compressor: None
- Rate: 48.000kHz
- Size: 16 bits
- Use: Stereo

❺ In the Settings area at the bottom, use the following settings for the Geometry tab:

a: If the video is larger than 720x480, you must crop it. For example, if the material is D1 (720x486), you need to crop six lines of information. Be sure to crop an even number of lines, such as four from the top and two from the bottom, to keep field order intact.

b: If the video isn't interlaced, such as 720x540 or 720x534, you can resize it. Set the Output size to 720x480.

6 Name the preset, and apply it to your clips.

7 Submit the job, and go do something else for a while.

Final Cut Pro Movie...What's My Name Again?

With Final Cut Pro 4, the Export menu underwent major changes. The options for exporting Final Cut Pro movies and QuickTime movies have changed names:

- **QuickTime Movie:** This is the same as a Final Cut Pro movie. The file is exported using the sequence settings for size, frame rate, compression, and so on.

- **Using QuickTime Conversion:** This opens all of the formats supported by QuickTime. By checking different boxes and pull-down menus, you can access several different formats including AVI, DV Stream, and Image Sequence. This is the method for getting a file out so it can be used in other applications or platforms that don't recognize or have the capacity to play back your video file with the Source Compression setting applied.

> AIFF
> FLC
> ✓ QuickTime Movie
> µLaw
> AVI
> Wave
> DV Stream
> Still Image
> Image Sequence
> MPEG–4
> System 7 Sound

When You Need Something Else

Compressor and the export options in Final Cut Pro are excellent; however, they aren't Windows-centric. Although the MPEG and QuickTime options play perfectly fine on PCs, you'll run into client bias for other formats. Consider the following programs for additional output needs:

Cleaner: This product has changed hands a few times but now resides with the capable discreet (www.discreet.com). Cleaner is a proven program that provides several output options. Formats that differentiate it from the Final Cut Pro built-in options include the following:

- RealMedia (OS 9 only; you'll have to boot or wait for RealMedia to release an OS X–capable encoder)

- Windows Media (because clients expect it, but please try to convert them to QuickTime–it rocks!)

- Kinoma (for playback on Palm OS devices…reminds us of QuickTime version 1)

- Video for Windows (the AVI format, but several more options than the QuickTime AVI Export module).

Squeeze: Squeeze is from the creators of the Sorenson codec, which is hands-down the best codec for CD-ROM and web delivery using QuickTime. The Sorenson Compression Suite offers an easy-to-use interface as well as the Sorenson professional codec, which adds variable bit rate (VBR) encoding and several other options. The formats of interest that it supports are as follows:

- QuickTime with Sorenson 3 VBR compression. This requires QuickTime 5 or newer to view.

- Flash Video format (FLV) for importing into Flash MX projects.

- Shockwave Format (SWF) for placement into web pages and viewing with the Flash plug-in.

- Windows Media is supposed to be coming soon (because some people like it).

Edit to Tape

The Edit to Tape function is a great mystery to some. "Why would I use it and how?" Edit to Tape allows you to perform timecode-accurate assemble and insert edits onto a linear tape. Remember, what type of edit you can perform is a function of your video deck, not of Final Cut Pro. Assemble edits let you start recording a specific spot in your show, but you need to record all the way to the end of the program. Insert edits allow you to replace just one shot or groups of shots, without having to rerecord the end of the show. And frame-accurate timecode insertion is a function of the deck, too. If you're in the market for a new deck, be sure to ask if these features are supported.

How (and Why) to Start at 1:00:00:00

If your show is going to hit air or even make that picky duplicator happy, your program should start at exactly at the one-hour mark. This means you need to start your bars and tone at 58:30:00, giving you enough time for slate and countdown. (By the way, countdowns are only needed for programs going to air; they just annoy duplicators.)

Most DVCam and Mini DV machines don't allow you to stripe timecode. To complicate things, Final Cut Pro doesn't allow you to stripe timecode onto your tape as you record your show (again, this is usually a function of the deck; they need a timecode-in capability).

Here's a trick we've used: The solution is to go "out of house" and have a friend with a deck that can generate timecode (or even a duplicator) create a couple of DV tapes with timecode that starts at 58:00:00. Now you can simply clone the timecode from your DV camera to your DV deck. Make sure you're connected FireWire to FireWire, and start the playback on the striped tape before you hit the Record button on the record deck. What you should get is a perfect clone of the timecode on the new tape.

You don't need to record the whole tapes. Just take it to a few minutes past the one-hour mark. Using the Edit to Tape command, you can target your In point at 58:30:00, perform an assemble edit, and you're golden.

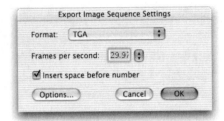

When All Else Fails

There's a sure-fire way to get your video out of Final Cut Pro and into another editing system: an image sequence. Essentially you output a still for every frame of video; you can then import these stills into another video application and work with them. This is one method that's sure to work, but it's a little cumbersome. Follow these steps:

❶ Mark a range in your clip or sequence by setting an In and an Out point.

❷ Choose File > Export > Using QuickTime Conversion

❸ From the Format drop-down menu, select Image Sequence.

❹ Click the Options button, and select a format and the appropriate frame rate. Targa is very popular with PC-based animators; PCT is more popular with Mac-based artists.

❺ Create a new folder, and specify the destination.

❻ Click OK.

Acknowledgments

My wife, Meghan, for her patience and love. You are an amazing person, and there are times I cannot believe you put up with my crazy jobs. As we move through life, I am grateful you are by my side.

My family for their support and guidance. All that I have, I owe to you. Thanks for all of the good advice and teaching throughout the years.

My coauthor, Abba Shapiro. Thanks for saying "yes" to this idea. Your insight and knowledge have made this a much better book.

—Richard Harrington

My wife, Lisa—my friend, my partner in life, my one true love. My sons, Daniel and Ian, who allow me to see all that is good and precious in this world. They are my life and my reason for being.

My parents Deena and Clarence Shapiro; I am lucky enough to follow in both of their footsteps. From my father, an engineer, I learned to understand and love technology. From my mother, a teacher, I learned to be a trainer and educator and to excite people with my passion for all things high-tech.

My coauthor, Richard. He started as a colleague and a collaborator and ended up a good friend. Without Richard, this book would not exist. He is a good teacher, a good project manager, and a very patient man.

—Abba Shapiro

The authors would like to thank the following for making this book possible:

Gary Adcock	Jeff Greenberg	Chris Phrommayon
George Annab	Scott Kelby	Paul Saccone
Frank Brogan	Ben Kozuch	Yan Shvalb
Dorothy Cox	Mac Design Magazine	Jessica Steigerwald
DV Magazine	Steve Martin	Paul Temme
Brandy Ernzen	Brian Meaney	Tom Wolsky
Final Cut Pro User Groups	Patty Montesion	

Updates

Want to receive e-mail news updates for *Final Cut Pro 4 On the Spot*? Send a blank e-mail to fcp4spot@news.cmpbooks.com. We will do our best to keep you informed of software updates and enhancements, new tips, and other FCP-related resources. Further, if you would like to contribute to the effort by reporting any errors, or by posting your own tips, please contact the authors at www.finalcutprohelp.com.

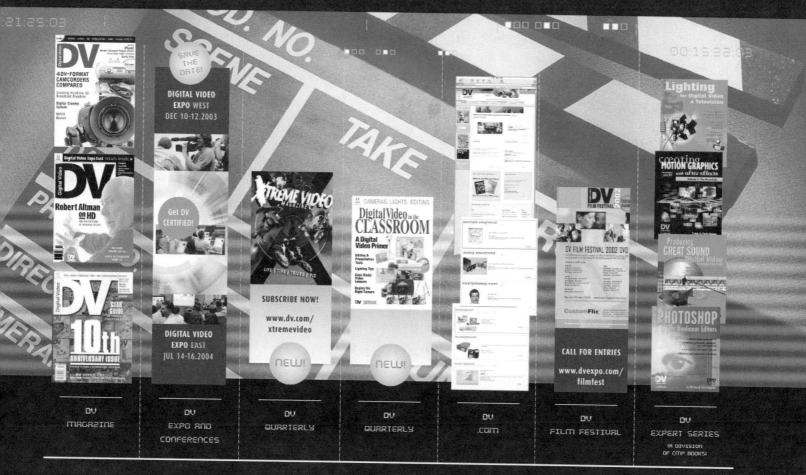

THE AUTHORITY ON DIGITAL VIDEO TECHNOLOGY

DV
MAGAZINE

DV
EXPO AND
CONFERENCES

DV
QUARTERLY

DV
QUARTERLY

DV
.COM

DV
FILM FESTIVAL

DV
EXPERT SERIES
(A DIVISION
OF CMP BOOKS)

INSPIRING AND EMPOWERING CREATIVITY

DV
Digital Video
Media Group

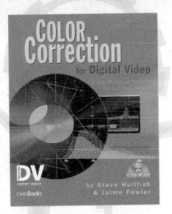

Color Correction for Digital Video
by Steve Hullfish & Jaime Fowler

Use desktop tools to improve your storytelling, deliver critical cues, and add impact to your video. Beginning w clear, concise description of color and perception theory, this full-color book shows you how to analyze c correction problems and solve them—whatever NLE or plug-in you use. Refine your skills with tutorials include secondary and spot corrections and stylized looks.

$49.95, 4-color, Softcover with CD-ROM, 202 pp, ISBN 1-57820-201-9

Nonlinear Editing
Storytelling, Aesthetics, & Craft
by Bryce Button

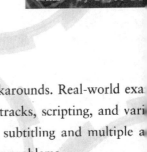

Build your aesthetic muscles with this application-agnostic guide to digital editing so you can make better decisions in the edit bay and in your career. The companion CD-ROM includes a treasure trove of valuable software, image files, tools, utilities, fonts, filters, and sounds.

$49.95, Softcover with CD-ROM, 523 pp, ISBN 1-57820-096-2

Working with DVD Studio Pro
by Mike Evangelist

Produce exciting, sophisticated DVD projects with fast, efficient solutions and workarounds. Real-world exa illustrate the most powerful features of the DVD medium, such as alternate soundtracks, scripting, and vari You learn how to master the more complex aspects of DVD authoring including subtitling and multiple a making discs that work on both widescreen and standard TVs, and solving replication problems.

$49.95, Softcover with DVD, 480 pp, ISBN 1-57820-217-5, Available February 2004